"THE ORIGINAL" COWLING SYSTEM

OF HAND STRENGTHENING EXERCISES

For All Musicians

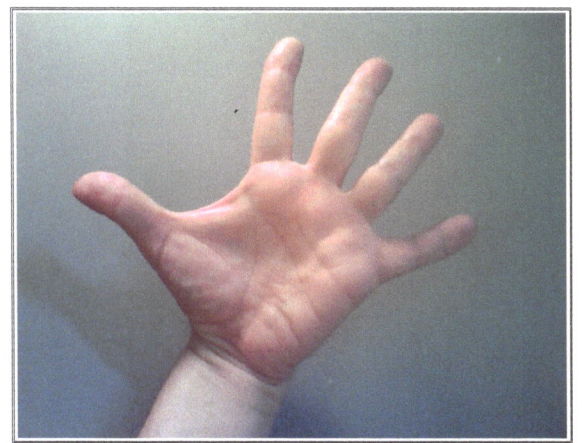
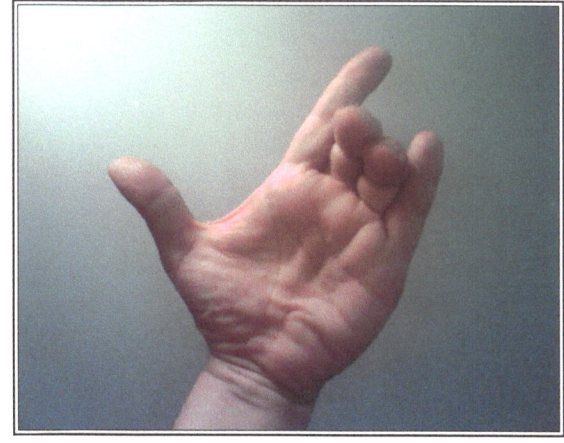

by E. J. PICKLES

NEW PHOTOGRAPHS AND ADDITIONAL MATERIAL
BY GEORGE HIRSCH

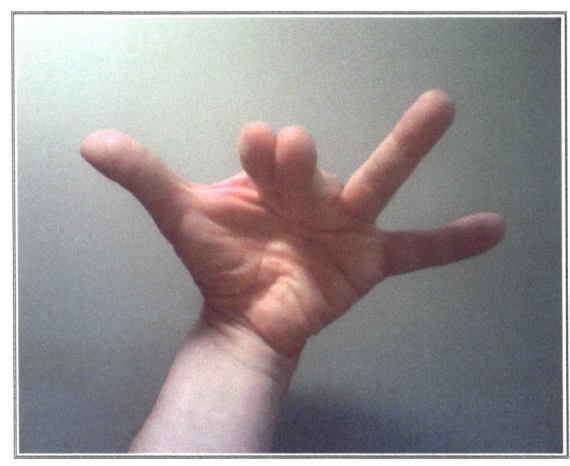
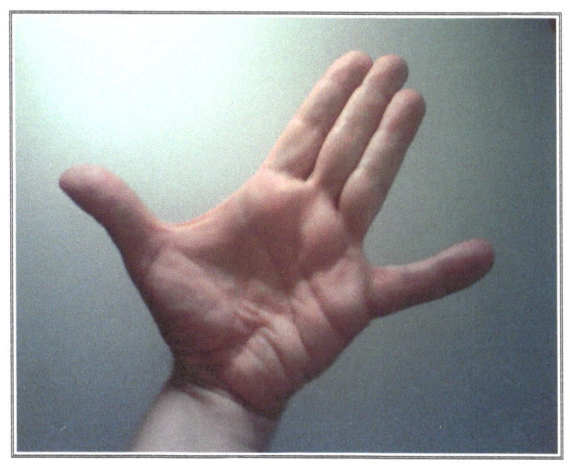

© 2007 BY GEORGE HIRSCH/ARTISTIC PRODUCTION SERVICES

"THE ORIGINAL" COWLING SYSTEM

"THE ORIGINAL" COWLING SYSTEM

OF

HAND STRENGTHENING EXERCISES

For All Musicians

BY E. J. PICKLES
{NEW PHOTOGRAPHS AND ADDITIONAL MATERIAL *by* GEORGE HIRSCH}

© 2007 BY GEORGE HIRSCH/ARTISTIC PRODUCTION SERVICES

© 2007 by George Hirsch

All rights reserved. No part of this book may be reproduced or transmitted in any form or by any means, graphic, electronic or mechanical, including but not limited to: photocopying, "scanning", recording, or by any other information storage and retrieval system, existing at the time of this writing or developed in the future, without the express written permission of the publisher or creator, except in the case of brief quotations excerpted for critical or review purposes.

Published 2007 by Artistic Production Services, NYC, NY

Contact Artistic Production Services at:

http://www.make-music-better.com/contact-us.html

Hardcopy version printed by CreateSpace, an Amazon.com company in the United States of America

Available from Amazon.com and other online stores

More information -- "The Original" Cowling System web page:

http://www.make-music-better.com/hand-strengthening-exercises-Cowling-System-5.html

ISBN 13: 978-0-615-17050-3

NOTICE/DISCLAIMER: This book is intended as a reference volume only. Not as a manual of, or for the purposes of physical therapy and/or physical rehabilitation of the hand or fingers. It is not intended as a substitute for professional diagnosis and recommendation in such matters. If you suspect that you have such a problem, including but not limited to "tendinitis", "sprains", "repetitive stress injury", "carpal tunnel syndrome", etc., we urge you to seek competent professional assistance in that regard. As with all exercise programs, you should seek your doctor's or physical or occupational therapist's or other professional's informed consent to ensure that this program is appropriate for your circumstances before embarking upon this program.

To my spouse, Anne, without whose untiring and complete support nothing would have been possible, and to any and every musician, artist and artisan, striving to make the products of their personal imaginations perceivable by others, and so create a better world, this book is dedicated.

TABLE OF CONTENTS

EDITOR'S FOREWORD BY: GEORGE HIRSCH   i

FOREWORD BY: E. J. PICKLES   iv

LESSON ONE:
   FOR DEVELOPING FLEXIBILITY OF THE FINGER JOINTS   1

HINTS ON SIGHT READING [ORIGINAL BONUS LESSON]   7

BASIC MUSIC THEORY [ORIGINAL BONUS LESSON]   9

LESSON TWO   11

LESSON THREE:
   FOR DEVELOPING INDEPENDENT MOVEMENT OF THE FINGERS   17

LESSON FOUR: [ORIGINAL BONUS LESSON]
   INTONATION - SOUND WAVE, FOR THE PIANO   21

LESSON FIVE:
   TO DEVELOP STRENGTH & INDEPENDENCE OF FINGERING   23

LESSON SIX:
   TO DEVELOP THE MUSCLES OF THE FOREARM   25

LESSON SIX A:
   FOR DEVELOPING THE UPPER ARM, SHOULDER
   AND CHEST MUSCLES   29

LESSON SEVEN:
   EXERCISING THE FIRST JOINTS   31

TABLE OF CONTENTS - CONT'D

LESSON EIGHT:
TO FURTHER DEVELOP INDEPENDENCE OF FINGERING   35

LESSON NINE:
COMBINED EXERCISE FOR THIRD JOINTS AND WRISTS   39

THE OCTAVE PLAYING EXERCISE   43

LESSON TEN:
POWER IN THE FOURTH FINGER! - FOR TRILLS, TURNS, SHAKES, AND EXTENDED MOVEMENTS FOR OCTAVE PLAYING   47

LESSON ELEVEN:
THUMB-UNDER EXCERCISE   51

CONGRATULATIONS!   55

"THE ORIGINAL" COWLING SYSTEM

Editor's Foreword

"When thought is directed to the movement of any muscle, the development of that muscle is accentuated in consequence."

- E. J. Pickles

It was sometime around the early '70's that this box ad began to appear in the back of the music magazines. *"FINGER MAGIC!"*, the ad proclaimed. The ad stated this system of exercise could dramatically increase the skill of a musician, maximize his practice time and take him or her to the next level, or levels beyond.

I was intrigued; here were testimonials from musicians who had not been able to get a breakthrough, but within weeks had achieved substantial, even virtuousic, power and skill. Skeptical though I was, I figured: "Hey, this could be useful."

So I filled out the enrollment form, sent it off to London, and eagerly awaited my first lesson. When I got the materials, I got to work and within about 3 days, from just the first exercise, the 'heaviness' and 'resistance' I always felt at higher tempos, had substantially **disappeared**. Hmmmmmm.......**NO 'WALL'** ! *It works!!*

With a metronome, I clocked some three-finger picking patterns at about a 50% increase in speed, and **THERE WAS LITTLE OR NO FATIGUE! Wow......**

So I kept the exercises up and within a few weeks, as promised. I attained a noticeable, stable overall increase in speed and power.

Coming forward to the present: Seeing that my original materials were deteriorating, I searched around to see if "The Cowling Institute" was still in existence, but to this date, I've found NO current info on Mr. Pickles and the Cowling Institute! [I saw some who still had and used some remnants of the material - My research did uncover the origin of the Cowling System is no later than 1904!]

So, I've gone ahead and replicated the complete text as originally published, and took new photos, to refresh and renew the presentation of these interesting, amazing and deadly effective exercises. ('Deadly effective' when done correctly, of course!).

I trust you'll be as totally amazed as I was when you experience the changes these exercises effect on your physical plant, your 'machine' [the body with which you manipulate your instrument].

Obviously, these exercises don't completely replace normal practice; BUT what these exercises DO do, is fully and completely exercise each critical internal muscle of the hand and forearm in a way that instrumental practice alone cannot:

Consider this: Most any scale or pattern exercise [Hanon, Czerny, etc.] on any instrument causes certain muscles to be fully contracted or extended for mere *fractions* of a second. However, in the Cowling System, precisely isolated muscles and tendons get worked for *10 or twelve seconds* at a time, in isolation and with full focused mental concentration. Then, they are worked again after several hours of rest and 'rebuild'. This, is *the* factor which does produce very rapid and maximum development.

So, given that the skills and patterns of movement are correctly assimilated through *correct* practice, the task of developing the "physical plant" can be accomplished as a separate activity. This reduces the overall task of attaining mastery by subdividing it into separate goals, each more easily attainable.

SPECIAL NOTE: Regarding those who need or are undergoing treatment or physical rehabilitation of the hands: While there are ample testimonials to the therapeutic effect of these exercises, you will note a continual warning in E. J. Pickles' general instructions that one is to cease exercising **immediately** at the first sign of actual pain, and to **never** "overdo it" in any case.

Therefore, the disclaimer in the front of the book is there for a reason; I don't want you hurting yourself; <u>You</u> have full and sole responsibility for your actions. So, if you have any doubt about what you are doing, STOP and read the material again. And use a dictionary to clear up any unfamiliar words.

Now: A few other suggestions which I have found to be of use:

0] Note that [except for lesson seven] these exercises are to be done **only one at a time, for a period of seven days on each exercise.** You can go through the whole book, doing a complete "rotation", then start over at lesson one again. The instructions are explicit in that regard, follow them.

a] Regarding **"complete thought", "complete attention",** etc.: There is nothing particularly "mystical", "spiritual", "meditative" or "hypnotic" about this - quite the contrary. I've found that you just need to direct what would be your <u>normal waking attention</u> to what you are doing. Say you were threading a needle - you'd put your <u>total</u> attention and concentration on it and you'd just ***do*** it. (Nothing against those other mental activities mentioned above, but they are just <u>not</u> part of the Cowling System.)

Now, It's possible that your mind will wander a bit. You don't have to frustrate yourself about it. Just as the body responds to any exercise physically, the mind responds in like manner, and starts to 'tighten up' (focus) as well, and you'll soon almost certainly be able to keep your attention totally on the exercise for the required ten or twelve seconds at a time, per digit. And you may even feel a real surge of exhilaration afterwards - a bonus.

You may also find that doing these exercises with full concentration makes them seem **easier**, and therefore, more fun.

b] Get an metronome if you don't have one [a $12 digital one is a good investment] and set it to 60 BPM, so it clicks or beeps once a second. Then you can concentrate, yet still count off the seconds accurately without having to shift your attention between your own hand and a clock face.

c] One more point which bears mentioning; and I hope you are not subject to the following regrettable circumstance, but: Stay away from those 'friends' who suggest you are wasting your time on this [hey-it's only ten minutes a day!!]. I've experienced that 'critics' of this system and many other things, are really exhibiting misunderstanding or deliberate ignorance - *to hell with them!* :)

So, do these exercises in your own peaceful, undisturbed space - and keep the discipline up. And if "they" happen to ask you how come your playing has gotten so much better so *quickly*, just smile.

And write me with your successes: As this community expands, I'd like to post your 'before-and-after' sound clips on our site, when possible.

I'm really excited about the Cowling system.

In fact, I even think the Cowling System could go so far as to change music itself - With so many more musicians not getting frustrated from lack of progress ('plateaus'), now being able to easily come up with their own new things, real good things - NOT getting stuck in the "familiar and easy rut", who knows where the next wonderful and interesting music will come from?

Will it be from you?

Please do stay in touch! [my contact data is in the back]

And now, for your edification, inspiration and enhancement we present.......

"THE ORIGINAL" COWLING SYSTEM!

Yours truly:

George Hirsch

"THE ORIGINAL" COWLING SYSTEM

Foreword
by: E. J. Pickles

When thought is directed to the movement of any muscle, the development of that muscle is accentuated in consequence. If a man determines to develop, for instance, a biceps muscle and simply fulfills the exercises prescribed by working that muscle according to directions given, his mind being on other things, the muscle does not develop so rapidly as if he concentrated his attention on that muscle.

There can be no doubt about this fact because it has been subjected to careful experiment, and the difference between merely mechanical movement, and movement with thought concentration, is all in favor of the latter.

Not long ago an instance was given of a Hindu, who is reputed to be the strongest man in the world, so far as weightlifting is concerned, He was able to lift these weights, not because his muscle was greater that that of the average weightlifter, but because, in developing his strength, he has concentrated his mind on the muscle to be developed.

This principle applied to the exercise of the system that you are learning is of the utmost importance. When practicing prescribed exercises, concentrate your mind upon the operation.

You will not only develop strength and flexibility of the member more rapidly, but the after-effects will be more certain.

Important Note:

It should be emphasized that no quick movements are involved in these exercises: The action should be slow and deliberate, avoiding any tendency to overdo. You will have the right idea if you operate as though pulling against a weak spring - if you think of a strong spring you will be applying too much resistance.

Carefully read the following pages, with the photos spread out before you in proper rotation, but do not attempt the actual exercise until you thoroughly understand what is intended.

It will be observed that these exercises commence with simple movements of one hand, assisted by the other hand.

These movements do not usually present any difficulty, and after the third position is reached, the service of the other hand is dispensed with.

Some students have difficulty in performing these latter movements correctly, and to such we would say persevere for two or three days, doing the best you can, after which it should be possible to place the fingers approximately as in photographs #4a, #5, #6, etc..

At the end of the week, most students are able to execute the final movements without the practice of the preliminary ones, [**i. e.: without the assistance of your other hand - ed**] although the fourth [little] finger may be troublesome.

A large percentage of students write to say that this first exercise has resulted in considerable improvement in speed and flexibility of fingering. In such cases, "binding ligaments" has been the cause of the difficulty, and this first exercise was the means of freeing those ligaments.

Firm and compact muscle can be developed by the use of dumbbells, corks and other mechanical devices, but firm and compact muscle is just what the instrumentalist does **NOT** want. Hence, no outside force whatsoever should be employed for the purpose of developing hand and fingers. What the instrumentalist needs is soft and flexible muscle of good quality, obtained by the gentle massage of the actual movement of the finger, plus thought concentration.

In 98% of cases, increase of stretch, improved responsiveness of the fingers, and a supple and strong wrist are the reward of serious and conscientious practice of the Cowling System.

Throughout the course we refer to the members of the hand as the 4th [little finger], 3rd, 2nd, 1st and thumb.

"THE ORIGINAL" COWLING SYSTEM

LESSON ONE

FOR DEVELOPING FLEXIBILITY OF THE FINGER JOINTS

[7 Photographs included: #'s, 1, 2, 3, 4, 4a, 5 & 6]

The photographs show the left hand - the exercises, however are to be performed first with the left hand, completing all the movements described, then with the right hand: but only by one hand at a time.

In the fingers are three joints - the joint near the nail - the middle joint - and the joint at the root of the finger - which we will term the first, middle and third joints, respectively.

In all the movements of this exercise the third joint must be kept well back and the finger bent ONLY from the MIDDLE joint. Keep the first joint as straight as possible.

FIRST POSITION: Hold the hand as in photo #1; fingers well back, an equal distance apart from each other, the hand being held wide open so that the "webbing" is being stretched to its full capacity, **but without hurting**, and retain for 10 seconds.

SECOND POSITION: as in photo #2: retain for 10 seconds.

THIRD POSITION: as in photo #3: holding the finger in position with the other hand [**if necessary**], and retaining for 10 seconds. Then repeat with each finger in turn, always keeping the other three fingers upright, and holding down for 10 seconds the finger you are bending.

A) After having tried this position with each finger in turn, with the left hand, repeat the cycle of operations, but this time simply <u>PLACE</u> the finger in the required position and try to retain for 10 seconds without holding with the other hand. Photo #4 illustrates the third finger retained in position without being held.

B) Then try the position illustrated in photo #4a, the two middle fingers being bent and the 1st and 4th kept straight. This is easier to perform if the 1st and 4th are pressed inwards on the other two, as a slight support, but it may be necessary to place them in position with the other hand. Retain for the usual 10 seconds.

C) Next, similarly bend the 1st and 4th while keeping straight the 2nd and 3rd and retain for 10 seconds

D) Then bend the 1st and 2nd fingers keeping the 3rd and 4th upright. Retain for 10 seconds.

E) Then bend the 3rd and 4th fingers, keeping the 1st and 2nd upright, retain for 10 seconds [These three movements: C, D, and E are not illustrated, but it is the same idea as in photo #4a, only with different fingers bent.]

F) Photo #5: Here is another combination; the 1st and 3rd fingers bent, 2nd and 4th upright. Retain for 10 seconds.

G) Photo #6: 2nd and 4th finger bent, 1st and 3rd upright.

Always begin by extending the hand as in photo #1, then close the fingers as in photo #2; , but after the second or third day it should not be necessary to hold down the fingers as described under **"THIRD POSITION"** and from photo #2, you should proceed through the movements as follows: **1, 2, A through G in rotation**, always retaining a position for 10 seconds.

After going through this series of movements from 1 through G with the left hand, change over to the right hand, and if not too tiring, repeat again with either hand [always one at a time].

This will occupy just over 10 minutes. The ideal is 10 minutes in the morning and ten minutes in the evening, but any hour of the day will do, so long as there is a considerable interval of rest between the two periods of exercising.

When the fingers are bent in the above manner and with thought concentration, the corresponding muscles are fully contracted, and the blood stream is drawn to the locality, bathing and nourishing muscle and nerve, and stretching each ligament in turn.

Note that photo #1 with this lesson is utilized in several other lessons also.

Mere movement of the finger is not sufficient - **ALL THE ATTENTION MUST BE CONCENTRATED ON THE EXERCISE** to attain the maximum benefit, but no force should be applied, and a certain amount of caution to avoid strain should be exercised initially.

Do not be tempted to exercise for longer than 10 minutes at any one period, and not for more than 20 minutes in one day. There is a physiological reason for this, and also for our rule that the exercise should be changed each week, upon the receipt of the next lesson.

"THE ORIGINAL" COWLING SYSTEM 3

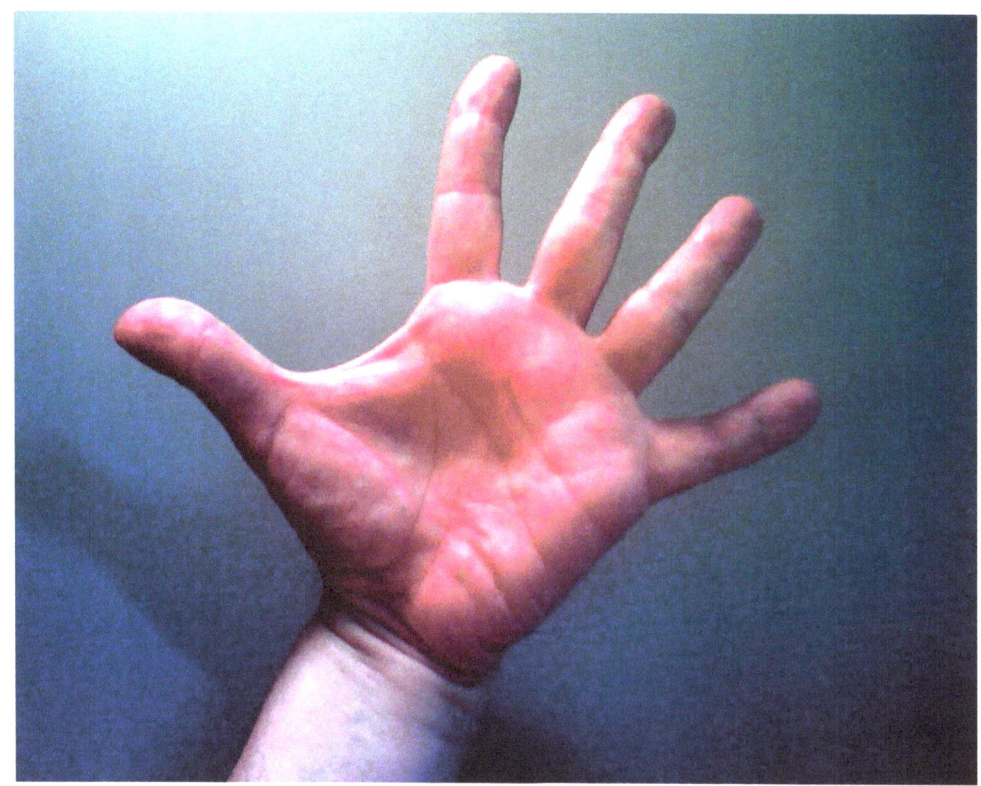

ONE - 1: "Starting Position"

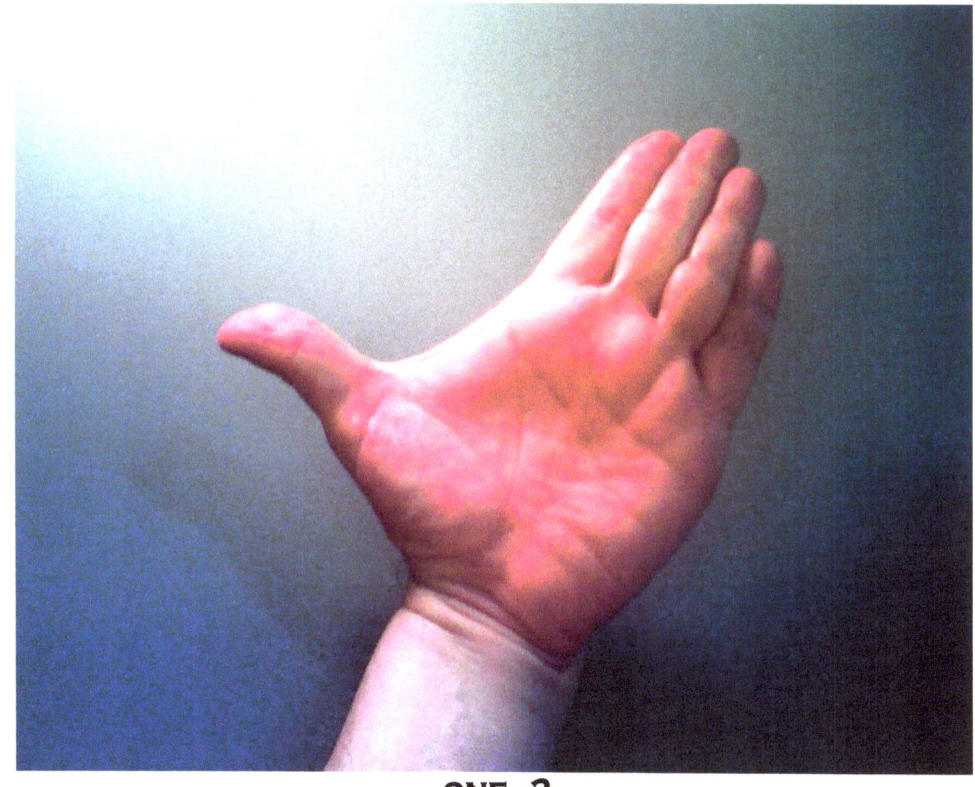

ONE - 2

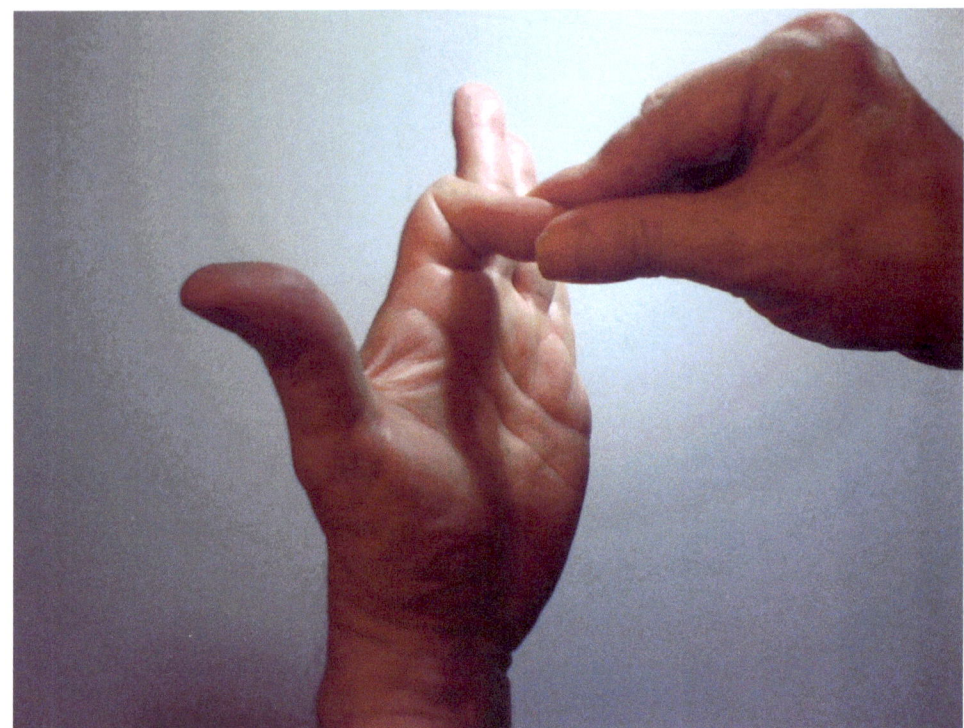

ONE - 3

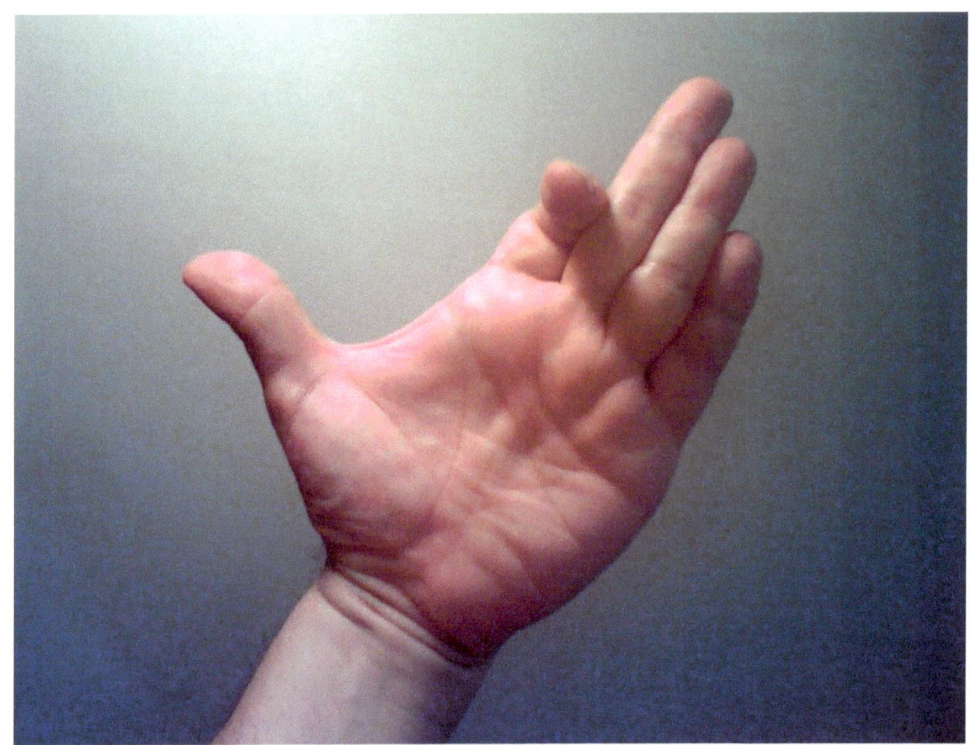

ONE - 4

"THE ORIGINAL" COWLING SYSTEM

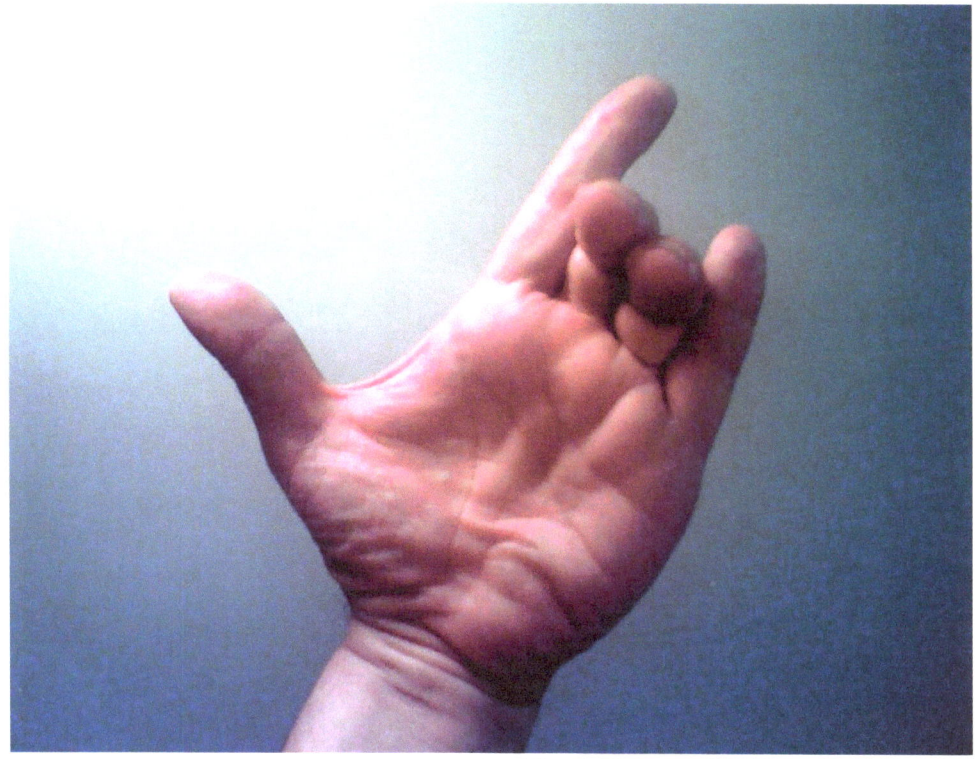

ONE - 4A

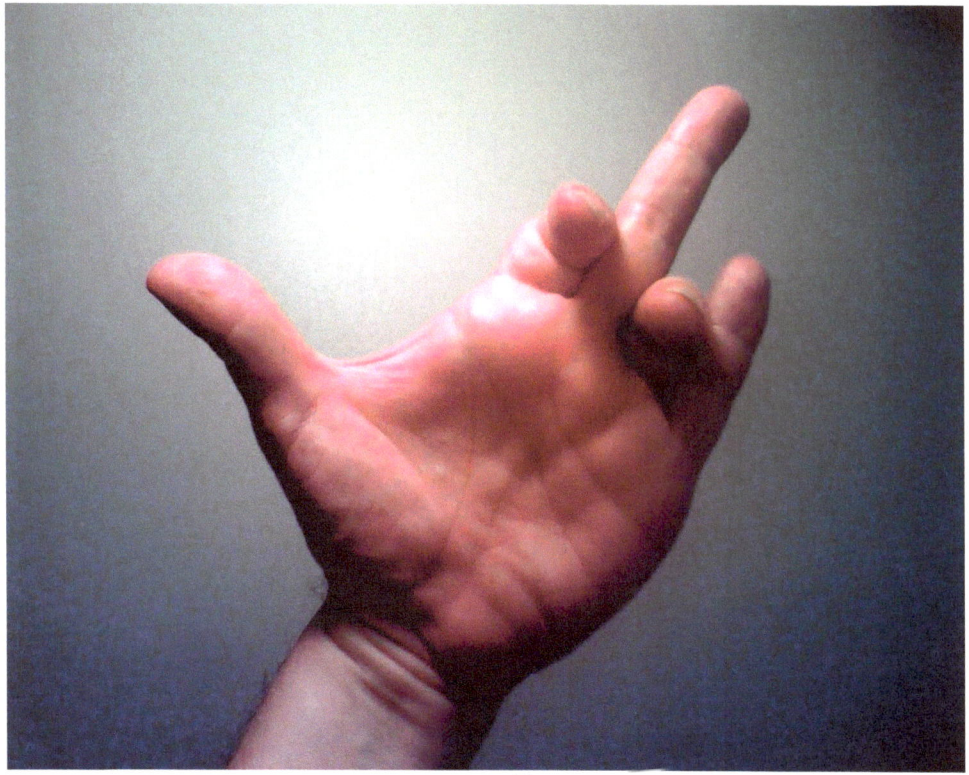

ONE - 5

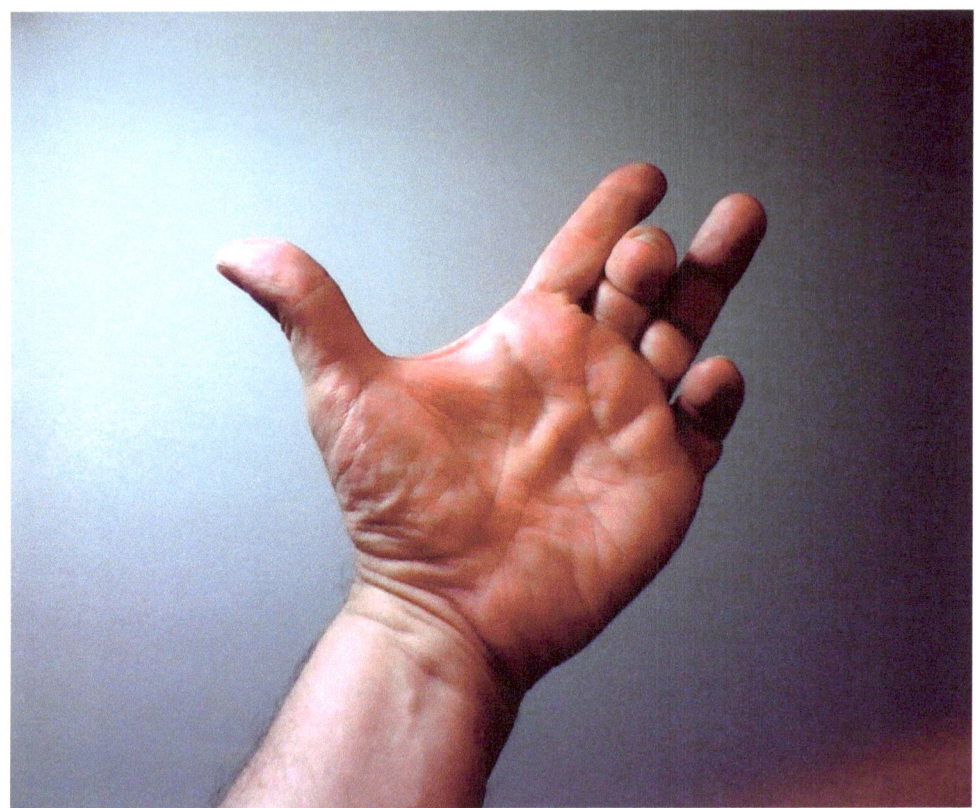

ONE - 6

HINTS ON SIGHT READING

There is no "royal road" to the acquisition of reading music at sight. The essentials are a knowledge of the Elements of Music and SYSTEMATIC PRACTICE, and PRACTICE is perhaps the more important.

If you will take the trouble to practice reading music for a few minutes daily, using the method described in the following pages, you can eventually arrive at the stage where you will be able to read simple music as easily as you read ordinary text.

It is of first importance that you should learn **all** the **major scales**, and the **harmonic and melodic minor scales**, in such a manner that any can be played instantly when named. Then the arpeggios of the common chord in each key should be learned, that is the tonic or key note, with its third and fifth - i. e.; C, E, G, C - in C Major - as the majority of florid passages are composed of scale passages and arpeggios.

You should also familiarize yourself with the appearance of the Chromatic Scales. Good musicians do not need to "READ" a chromatic scale, they learn to recognize one at a glance - so that it is necessary only to read the first and final notes. As the average person, when reading ordinary text does not distinguish each letter but 'sees' the word as a whole, so will you read music with a little intelligent practice.

Make special note of the following practice:

EXERCISE A; Take an old sheet of any music, and write under each note the name of that note, for example: G-A-B-F# etc., using a pencil and writing lightly so that it can be erased. Do this not only with single note music [melody] but also with chords, commencing with the lowest note and spelling out the chord, for example:

G
E
C

If done systematically for ten minutes or more every day, this alone will effect a wonderful improvement in a very few weeks.

EXERCISE B: In addition, you should play at least one short piece of new music every day - music that you do not know, and easy music initially, but afterwards more florid music with ledger lines.

[For pianists, hymn tunes and chants, *Kuhlau's* and *Clementi's* Sonatinas and *Bertini's Easy Studies* are recommended. For violinists, *Kayser's* and *Maza's* Studies. For cellists, *Kummer's* and *Lee's* Duets.]

"THE ORIGINAL" COWLING SYSTEM

BASIC MUSIC THEORY

The technical names of the degrees of the major scale:

[in the key of C:]

1st note;	*Tonic/Key Note*	C
2nd note;	*Supertonic*	D
3rd note;	*Mediant*	E
4th note;	*Subdominant*	F
5th note;	*Dominant*	G
6th note;	*Submediant*	A
7th note;	*Leading Tone*	B
8th note;	*Octave*	C

In the Major Keys, the last sharp added is always the Leading Tone and the last flat added is always the Subdominant. For example, in the key of G, F# [the only sharp] is the Leading Tone; in the key of D, C# [the last sharp added] is the Leading Tone.

In the Minor keys, the, the last sharp added is always the Supertonic, and the last flat added is always the Submediant, For example, in the key of E minor, F# [the only sharp] is the Supertonic; and in the key of B minor, C# [the last sharp added] is the Supertonic.

The relative minor of a major scale commences on the third below the major tonic and has the same key signature. For example; the relative minor of the key of C is A minor.

If music theory is a new subject to you, carefully study the examples, and work out the rest for yourself in all the major and minor keys.

Every sharp key is a fifth higher than the previous key: C is the natural key, having no flats or sharps. The key of G has one sharp [F#, the leading tone], and commences an fifth higher than C. D has two sharps [C# is the leading tone], and commences a fifth higher than G, or one string higher on the violin or cello. A has three sharps [G# is the Leading Tone] and in one string higher than D, and so on.

The consecutive order of the Major Keys is easily memorized by learning the following mnenonical sentences:

SHARPS: **G**ood **D**ays **A**re **E**ver **B**eing **F#**ound
FLATS: **F**lowers **Bb**loom **Eb**arly **Ab**nd **Db**ecay **Gb**radually

"THE ORIGINAL" COWLING SYSTEM

The initial letters of the words tell you the name of the key, and the consecutive ORDER of the words indicates how many sharps or flats there are in that key, for example:

SHARPS: The key of **G** - [initial of 1st word] has **1 sharp**
The key of **D** - [initial of 2nd word] has **2 sharps**
The key of **A** - [initial of 3rd word] has **3 sharps** - and so on

FLATS: The key of **F** - [initial of 1st word] has **1 flat**
The key of **Bb** - [initial of 2nd word] has **2 flats**
The key of **Eb** - [initial of 3rd word] has **3 flats** - and so on

The knowledge of the key in which the composition is written is a great help in sight-reading. Look at the key signature; If, for example, it is in three flats you know that it is either Eb major or C minor. The mnemonical sentence tell you this. then look at the last note **IN THE BASS** - if a chord, or the lowest note. **THIS LAST NOTE IS ALWAYS* THE KEY NOTE.**

Work out a dozen examples for yourself by means of these sentences and you will in the future be able to name the key at a glance.

---

*Editor's note: At the time of this writing, C. 1904, this was almost always the case - not so today - various pop, rock and country songs now use 'third-in-the-bass', 'fifth-in-the-bass' voicings & 'passing tones', etc..
There is no substitute for good, accurate listening and knowledge - Know 'the rules' so well that you can use them and also break them when needed. (As, for example, J. S. Bach did!)

"THE ORIGINAL" COWLING SYSTEM

LESSON TWO

This exercise is somewhat strenuous, and unless you are quite strong and robust, it is advisable to proceed with caution at the outset.

Read the instructions carefully, perhaps twice through, before attempting the actual exercise - with the photographs spread out in front of you - and follow the movements mentally. Remember that much depends on the mental attitude while practicing these exercises. To do them perfunctorily, allowing the mind to wander to other matters, is to lose much of their value.

When you reach position #9, do not clench the hand very tightly for the first two or three days, but after that, assuming you are quite strong and there had been no injury to the hand, clench it as tightly as you can without causing pain, the thumb pressing against the side of the first finger. on the long bone [third phalange] of that member.

There is a ligament which encircles the wrist and when elasticity of this ligament is developed, greater freedom of movement at one ensues.

The photos show the left hand, The exercises however are to be practiced first with the left hand, completing all the movements the with the right hand - **ONE HAND AT A TIME.**

Care most be taken that the fingers, hand and wrist, are not unduly strained by "putting too much" into the exercise. The movements should be done gently at first, especially if the student is not very robust, and all are to be performed without the aid of the other hand.

The movements should contract the muscles to the fullest possible extend, **CLOSE ATTENTION BEING GIVEN TO WHAT IS BEING DONE**. The mind must be centered upon the fingers and wrists and on the varying positions they are made to assume.

IN THIS EXERCISE THERE IS NO STOP WHATEVER - it is a continuous movement, and it differs in this respect from other exercises.

LESSON TWO, CONT'D

Bend the arm, with the elbow pointing to the ground and almost touching the side of the chest, the fingers pointing upwards, the hand being held about a foot from the front of the shoulder.

As in photo **One - 1: "Starting Position"**, hold the hand in this position with the fingers well back and equally wide apart.

Slightly bend the fingers as in photo **Two - 7**, still keeping them equally wide apart. Then proceed to the position shown in photo **Two - 8**, endeavoring to keep the fingers from touching.

Then clench the hand tightly, as in photo **Two - 9**. It is very important that the hand should be very tightly clenched, all the attention being concentrated upon the operation, and the hand retained in that position for 10 seconds.

Open the hand smartly, assuming again the position shown in **One - 1: "Starting Position"**. Then bend the hand from the wrist towards you, with fingers pointing to the shoulder. as in photo **Two - 11**, then -

Turn the hand 'round, as far as possible, away from the body, as in photo **Two - 10**, keeping the wrist bent as much as possible.

Still keeping the wrist well bent, bring the hand round towards you as far as possible, as in photo **Two - 11**, finishing by opening the hand 'smartly' [with a 'snap'], back to the original position as in photo **One - 1: "Starting Position"**, fingers well back, then repeat.

Commence the exercise each time at **#1**, finishing with **#11**. #1 through #11 is a complete movement. **[ed. note - you will probably feel and see the blood flush into your forearm and hand at the completion of the movement.]**

Practice three to six complete movements with the left hand and then three to six movements with the right hand, repeating alternately for a 10 minute period in the morning, and a ten minute period at night.

Do this exercise slowly at first, but when it is properly understood, the speed may be increased. One complete movement should occupy about 20 seconds.

Remember that when the muscles are fully contracted, the impure blood is expelled. When the muscles are relaxed, every fiber is bathed with new blood and this nourishes the muscle.

The building up of the muscle takes place during the intervals of rest, that is - after the end of the exercise period, making the movement more easy *after* each set.

The previous exercise should now be discontinued.

"THE ORIGINAL" COWLING SYSTEM

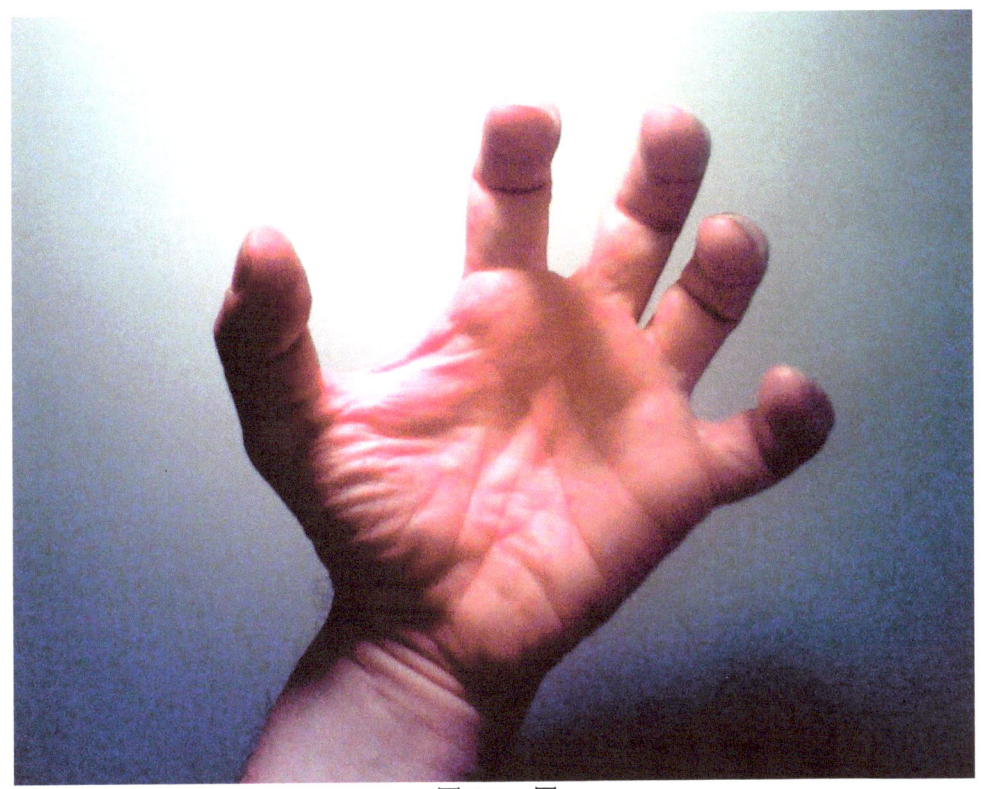

Two - 7

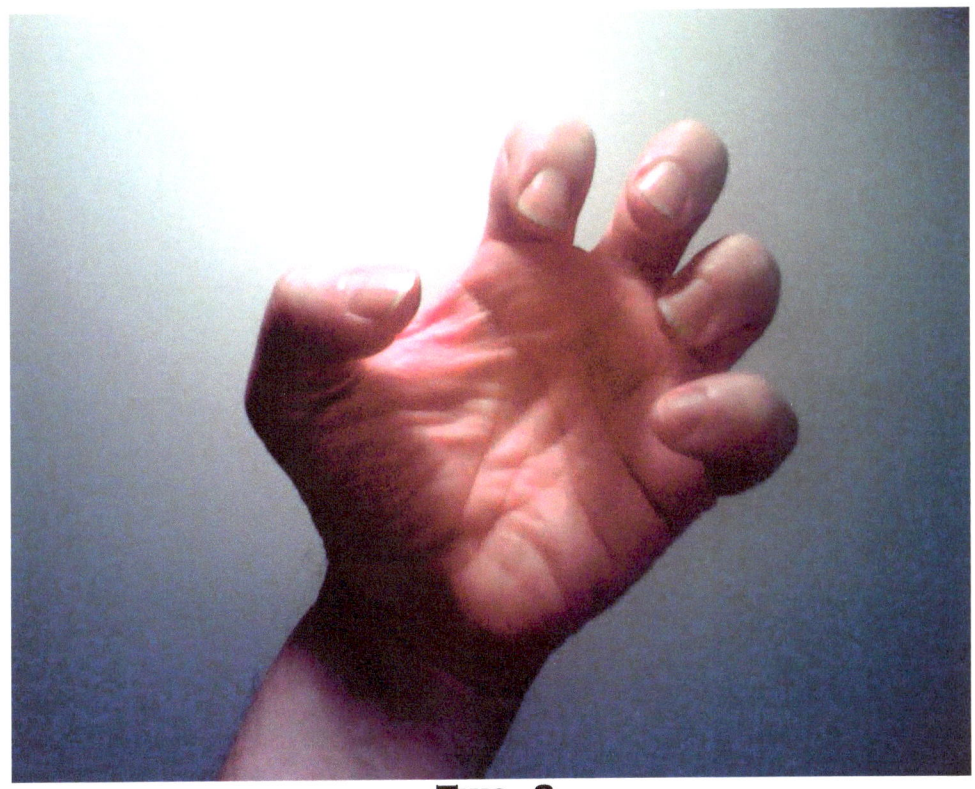

Two - 8

14   "THE ORIGINAL" COWLING SYSTEM

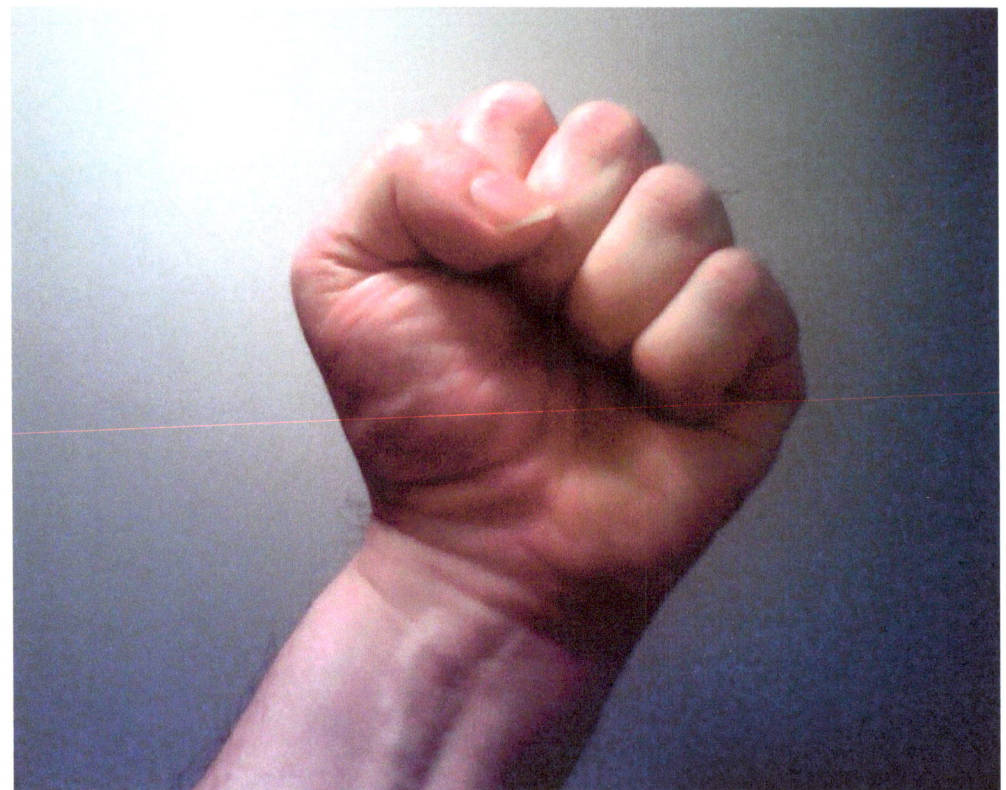

TWO - 9

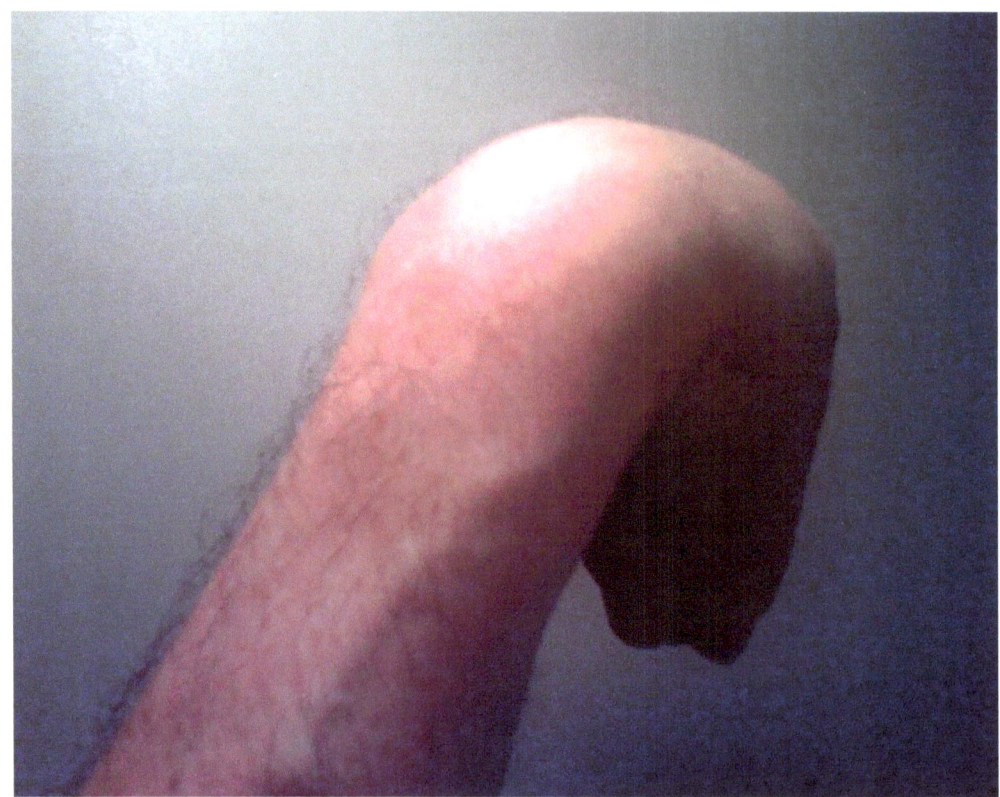

TWO - 10

"THE ORIGINAL" COWLING SYSTEM 15

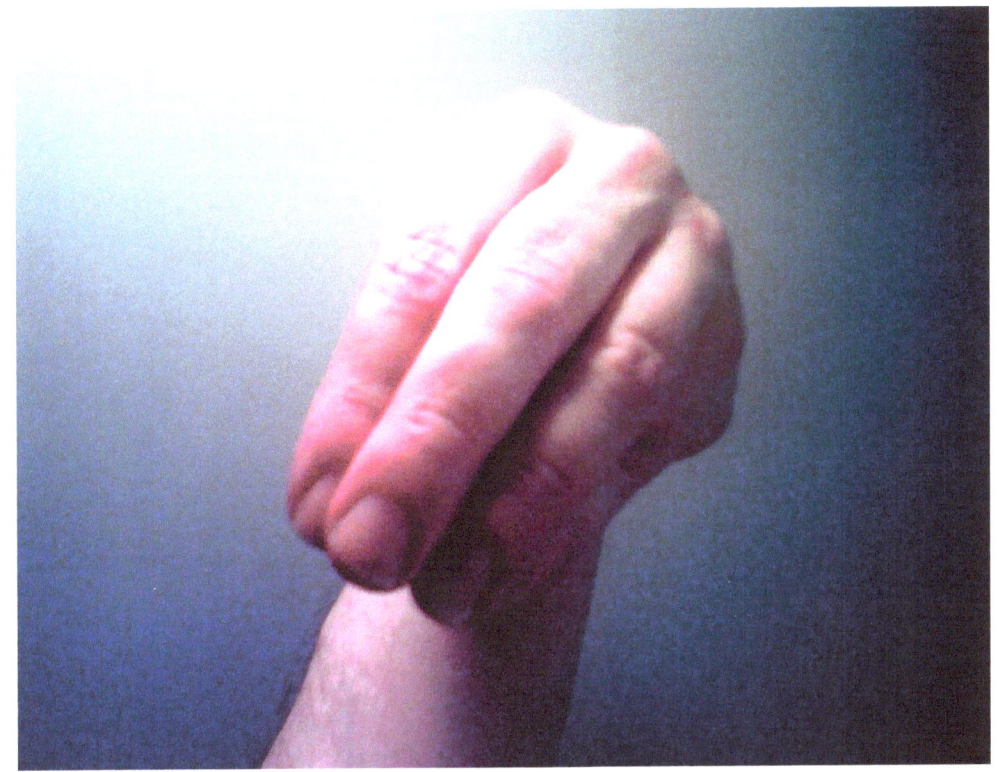

TWO — 11

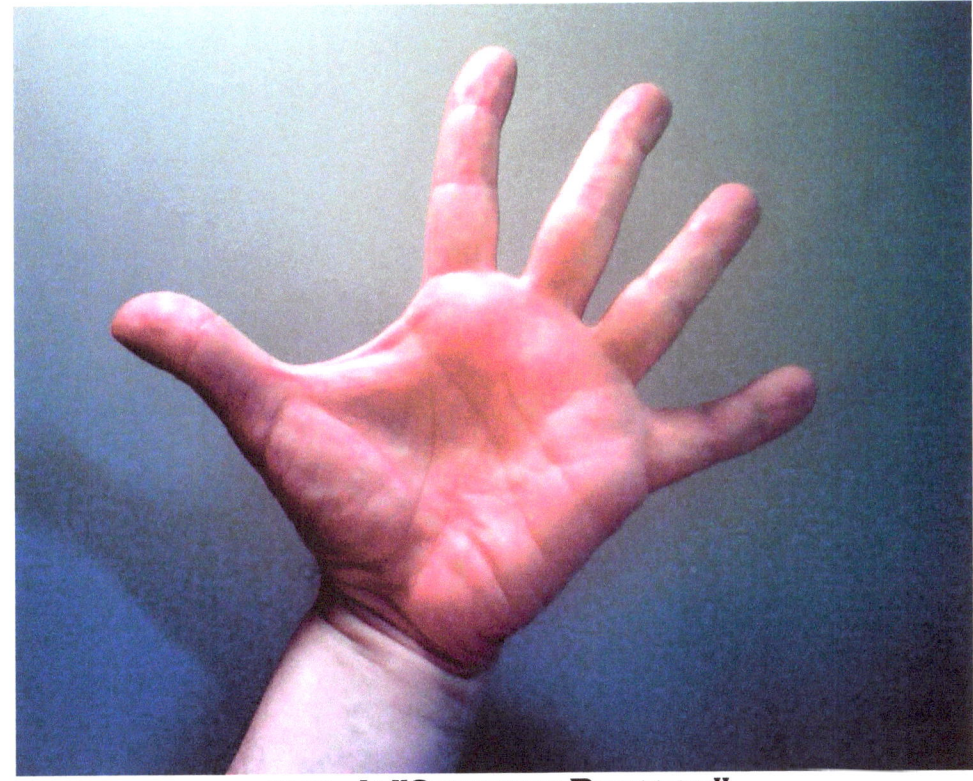

ONE - 1: "STARTING POSITION"

"THE ORIGINAL" COWLING SYSTEM

LESSON THREE

FOR DEVELOPING INDEPENDENT MOVEMENT OF THE FINGERS

6 PHOTOGRAPHS: NO'S. 1-12-13-14-15-16
[PHOTOGRAPH 1 FROM LESSON ONE]

The photographs show the left hand. The exercises however are to be practiced first with the left hand, beginning at photo #1, then with the right hand. Only one hand at a time - never both together. [See paragraph in all caps, below].

Practice for 10 minutes at night and 10 minutes in the morning.

All the attention should be concentrated on the various movements - the mere working of the fingers is not sufficient - in order to obtain the best results. Each movement should involve the fullest possible contractions.

If you are not very robust commence with 5 minutes practice night and morning, and increase to ten minutes on the third day.

In the fingers are three joints, the joint near the nail, the middle joint, and the joint at the root of the finger. which we will term the first, middle and third joints respectively.

The first or starting position is shown in photo **#1**, fingers well back, an equal distance apart from each other, the hand being held wide open so that the "webbing" is being slightly stretched.

Hold this position for 10 seconds, *but never so strenuously as to hurt the webbing.*

Then immediately change to the **second position** as in photo **#12**, the fingers being fully bent and held for 10 seconds.

Next, change to the **third position**, as shown in photo **#13**, retaining this also for 10 seconds.

And finally the **fourth position**, as shown in photo **#14**, holding this similarly for 10 seconds.

Now do these movements with the right hand, then again with the left, then again with the right, until you have exercised for ten minutes, by which time there should be a feeling of mild tiredness in the fingers.

NOTE THAT PHOTOS #15 AND #16 DO NOT INDICATE POSITIONS: THEY ARE MERELY SIDE VIEWS OF THE HAND, SHOWING THE CORRECT AND INCORRECT POSITIONS. PHOTOGRAPH #15 SHOWS THE FINGERS CORRECTLY FLEXED, FROM THE THIRD JOINT, BUT KEPT QUITE STRAIGHT IN THEMSELVES. PHOTOGRAPH #16 SHOWS THE FINGERS INCORRECTLY FLEXED, THE FINGERS NOT BEING KEPT STRAIGHT IN THEMSELVES.

In photo #12 [second position], the fingers not flexed cannot be kept **quite** upright.

In photo #13 [third position], the fingers not flexed **can** be kept **nearly** upright.

In photo #14 [fourth position], the fingers not flexed **can** be kept **quite** upright.

Car must be taken not to overstrain, either by exercising too strenuously or by exceeding the time specified.

The previous exercise should now be discontinued and replaced by this exercise.

"THE ORIGINAL" COWLING SYSTEM 19

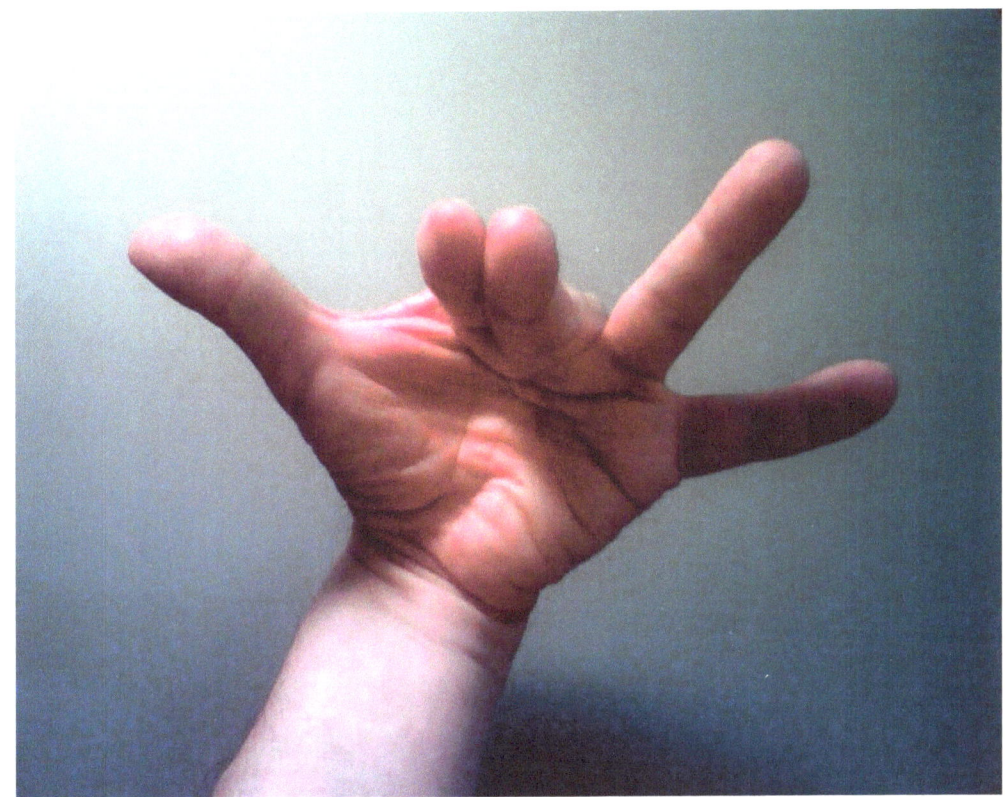

THREE - 12

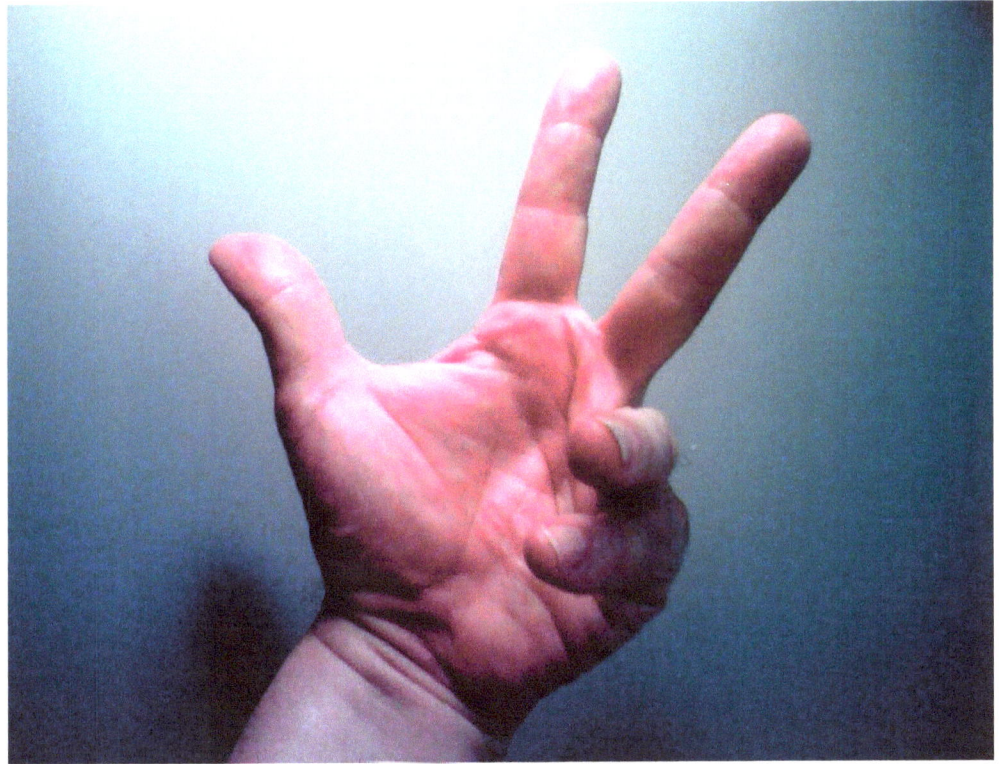

THREE - 13

20 "THE ORIGINAL" COWLING SYSTEM

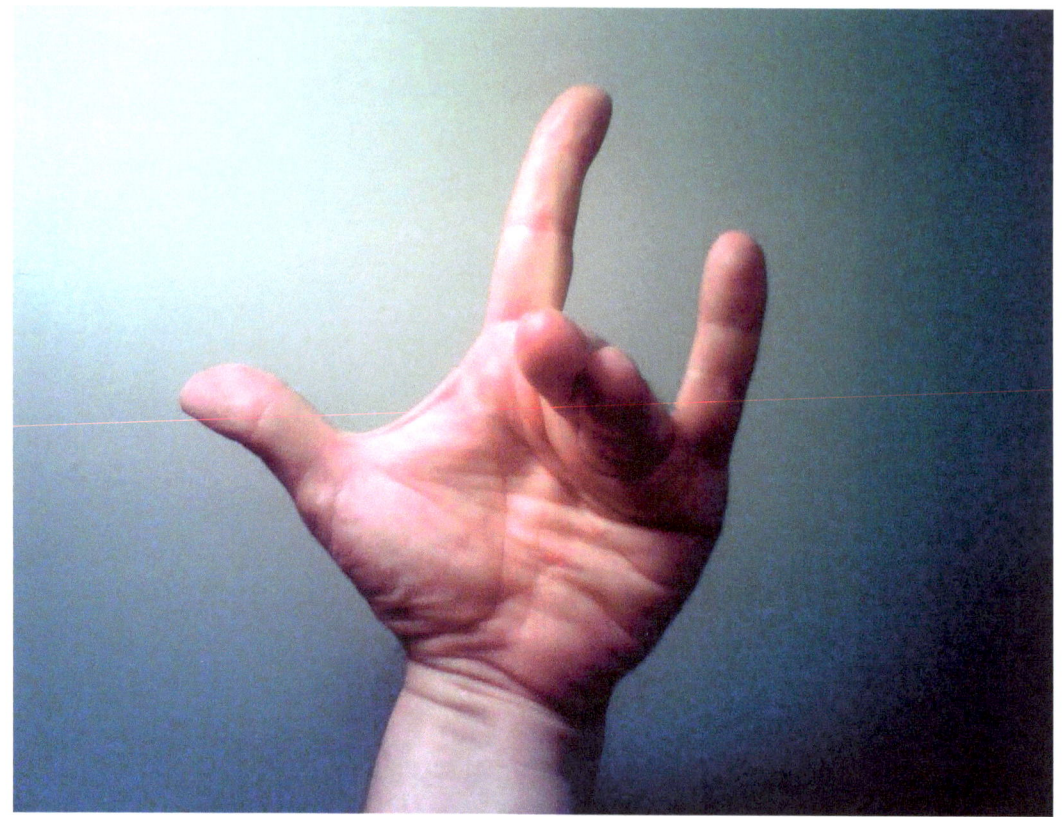

THREE – 14

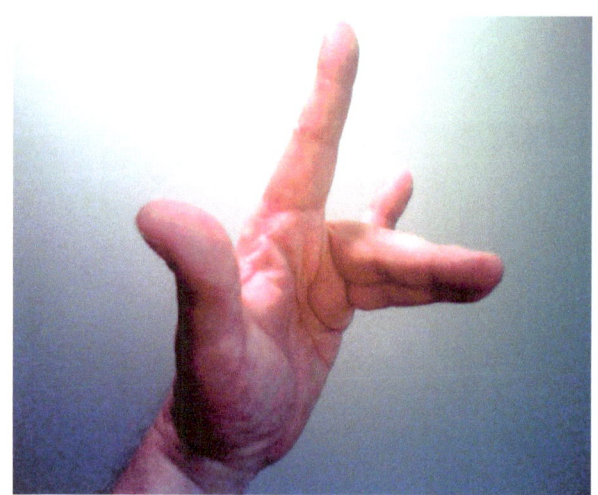

[CORRECT]

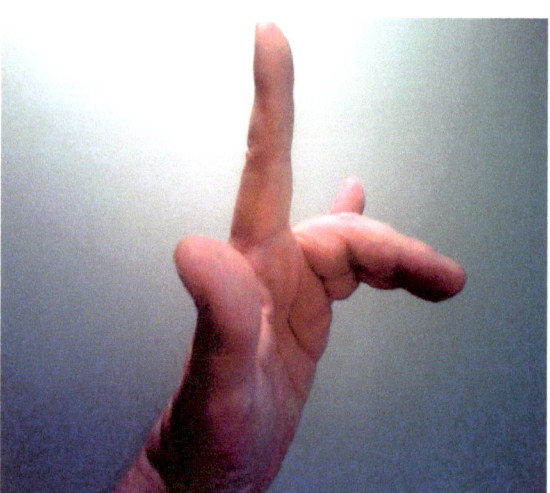

[INCORRECT]

"THE ORIGINAL" COWLING SYSTEM

LESSON FOUR

INTONATION - SOUND WAVE
For the Piano

Seated at the piano, strike an octave somewhere about the center of the keyboard. The two notes should be struck exactly together - not one after the other - and held until the sound has died away.

If the octave is not quite true - and there are generally one or two on most pianos which are not true - the ear can be trained to detect a distinct 'beat', by listening intently.

The string of a musical instrument vibrates not only throughout its entire length, but also in equal parts, each part producing a different note, which is called the harmonic. The fundamental note [**entire string length**] is strongest, and the higher the harmonics are [**shorter vibrating segments of the entire string**] the weaker they become.

These harmonics are absolutely essential to a musical tone - the more there are in a musical tone, the more 'brilliant' that tone is. The difference between 'tone' and 'noise' is that in noise there are no harmonics. These harmonics are also called "upper partials" or "overtones", and if an octave is not quite correct, some of these upper partials clash and create 'beats'.

If the octave is much out of tune, the dissimilar frequencies will produce a harsh and jarring effect. If not very much out of tune, by listening intently [while holding both notes down] a number of strong and rapid pulsations or 'beats' will be heard. If the octave is only slightly out of tune, mere undulations or waves will be audible. If in perfect tune, a steady and continuous note will be heard with no waves or beats.

The interval of an octave is divided into 12 semitones - a perfect fifth spans 7 semitones, a major third spans 4 semitones. The fifth that is produced in Nature [**equivalent to "just intonation"**], and the fifth of 7 semitones on the piano [**"equal temperament"**] are not exactly the same; For a perfect fifth, the difference amounts to 2 cents [**2%**] of a semitone sharp on the piano. Nature's major third is 14 cents [**14%**] flat compared to it's corresponding major third on the piano. Therefore the fifth on the piano winds up slightly sharpened and the third slightly flattened from "Just Intonation" to provide equal temperament for every key signature,

LESSON 4 - CONT'D

As mentioned previously, a musical sound is not a simple tone but one comprising several tones. If the note C on the piano is struck and held down, the fundamental will be heard first, and then, very faintly other notes or 'upper partials' will be perceivable, as indicated here:

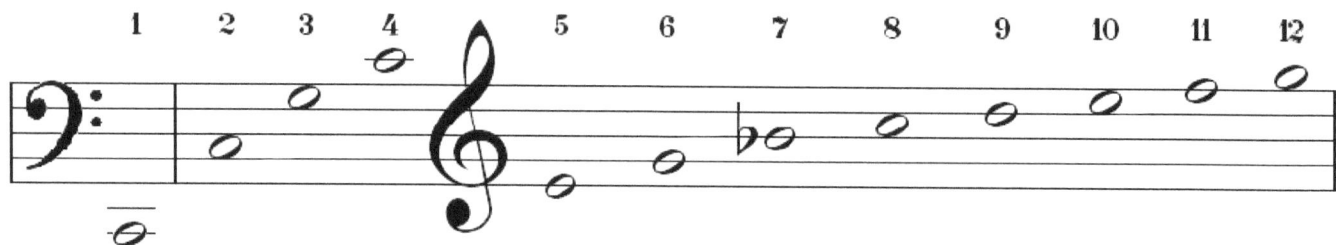

The notes numbered 2 and 4, being octaves of a fundamental note, cannot be detected by the unaided ear, but numbers 3, 5 and 6 can easily be heard. All these upper partials are faintly generated along with the fundamental tone and it is the presence of the these which imparts the 'brilliancy' and particular timbre [**quality and identity of sound**] to a musical note.

If the student's piano is absolutely in tune, there will be no waves or 'beats' heard when an octave is played, but if [as is often the case] an octave is not quite in tune, a distinct wave or 'beating' is audible, and the more the notes are out of tune, the faster the beating will be.

Contrarily, on a piano which is in perfect tune, beats will occur when any perfect fifth is played. As explained, above, "Nature's" perfect fifth and fifth represented by the interval of seven semitones on the piano, do not quite agree, and this difference is manifested by the waves or beats heard on the piano. A piano tuner has to tune the fifths about two beats per second flatter than the perfect, or Nature's fifth.

This all applies to the major third, with the following difference; it must be sharpened instead of flattened; Nature's major third is 3.86 equal-tempered semitones, as compared with the 4.00 equal-tempered semitones of the piano.

It would be impossible to tune a piano by judging the pitch as a violinist does. The sound-wave system is the method used by the piano tuner.

The student may find that he is unable to detect these waves or beats at the outset, but a little practice along the lines indicated, and also in attempting to detect all the upper partials enumerated above, will develop a fine and keen ear for pitch, without which, many an otherwise talented instrumentalist or vocalist remains in obscurity.

LESSON 5

TO DEVELOP STRENGTH & INDEPENDENCE OF FINGERING

[TWO PHOTOGRAPHS: # 17 & #18]

The photographs show the left hand, but the exercises are to be practiced first with the left hand, then with the right hand - one hand at a time.

FIRST POSITION: as in photo **#17** [fingers well back] retain this position for 5 seconds,

Then change to the **SECOND POSITION** as in photo **#18**, the three fingers bent down as far as possible; keep them straight at the middle joint, and bend only from the palm of the hand.

Keep the first finger as upright as possible. Retain this position for 10 seconds.

Do this five times with the left hand, then 5 times with the right, first as shown in the photos, then - bending the *other* three fingers and keeping the *little finger* upright.

REPEAT for ten minutes, twice daily, the two periods of exercise separated by at least one hour.

As given in the earlier lessons, the instructions regarding concentrating attention and care to avoid strain should be strictly observed.

24   "THE ORIGINAL" COWLING SYSTEM

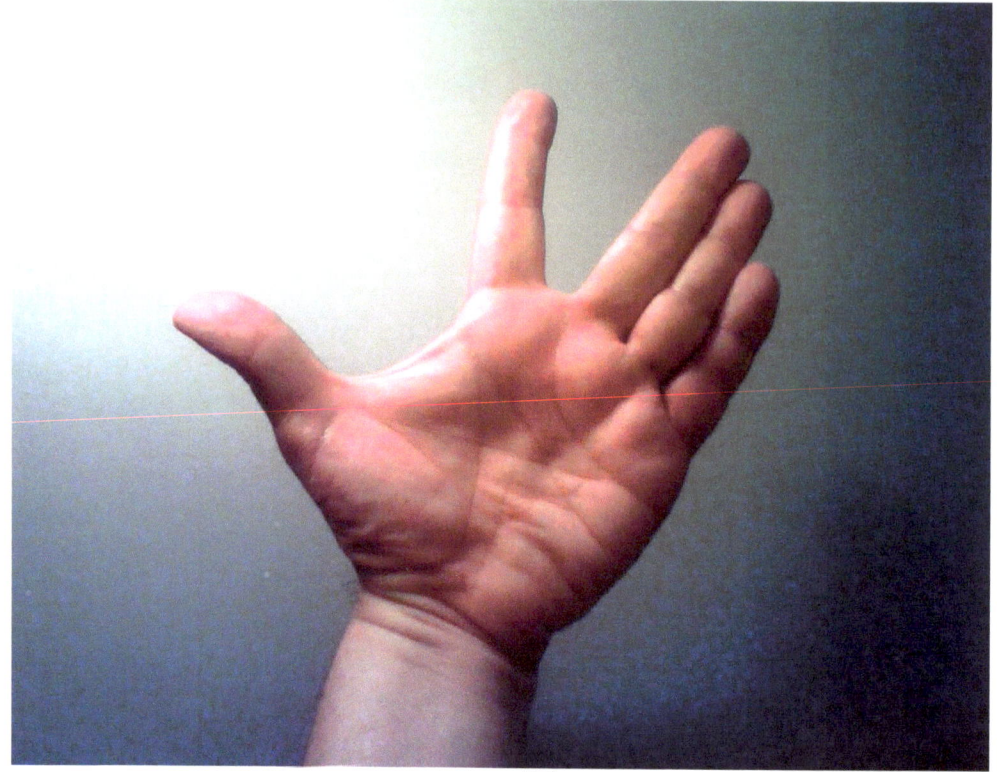

FIVE - 17

FIVE - 18

"THE ORIGINAL" COWLING SYSTEM   25

LESSON SIX

TO DEVELOP THE MUSCLES OF THE FOREARM

[Three Photographs: #'s 19, 20 & 21]

The photographs show the left hand, but the movements are to be performed first with the left hand, then with the right, one hand at a time, not both together.

It is an observable fact that the fingers cannot be under perfect control unless the muscles which actuate them are in a clean and healthy condition. As these muscles are situated in the forearm, the following exercise is a necessary support to any scheme for the development of the fingers, and it is given at this stage in order that the student may have a rest and change from actual finger movements. It is of course just as important as any other exercise in this series, and should be practiced with similar diligence.

Take a piece of thick paper, doubling it once or twice so that it will provide a good grip, and hold it between the thumb and first finger of the left hand. Place the hand as in photo **#19**, hand held as far back as possible, and retain this position for a count of ten seconds.

Concentrating all the attention, bring the hand slowly to the position indicated in photo **#20**, fingers almost touching the shoulder, and hold this position for ten seconds.

Then return to the starting position as in photo **#19**, holding for ten seconds - repeat the entire cycle six or seven times with the left hand, then proceed in the exact same manner with the other hand.

Practice this exercise with the arm slightly bent at the elbow, as in photo **#20**, and then with the arm quite straight, as in photo **#21**. **[editors note: Photo 21 shows how the hand would look from your 'point of view'.]** When practicing with arm straight, the fingers will of course be some distance from the shoulder.

Alternate with the left and right hand, each hand done firstly with arm bent and then done with arm straight [**2 x 6 or 7 'reps' each hand = 12 or 14 'reps' total**]. This will comprise two periods of ten minutes each, and these periods should be separated by at least two hours if possible.

The previous exercise should now be discontinued. The instructions regarding concentrating the mind upon the movements, and care to avoid strain, as given in all earlier lessons, should be strictly observed and followed.

26 "THE ORIGINAL" COWLING SYSTEM

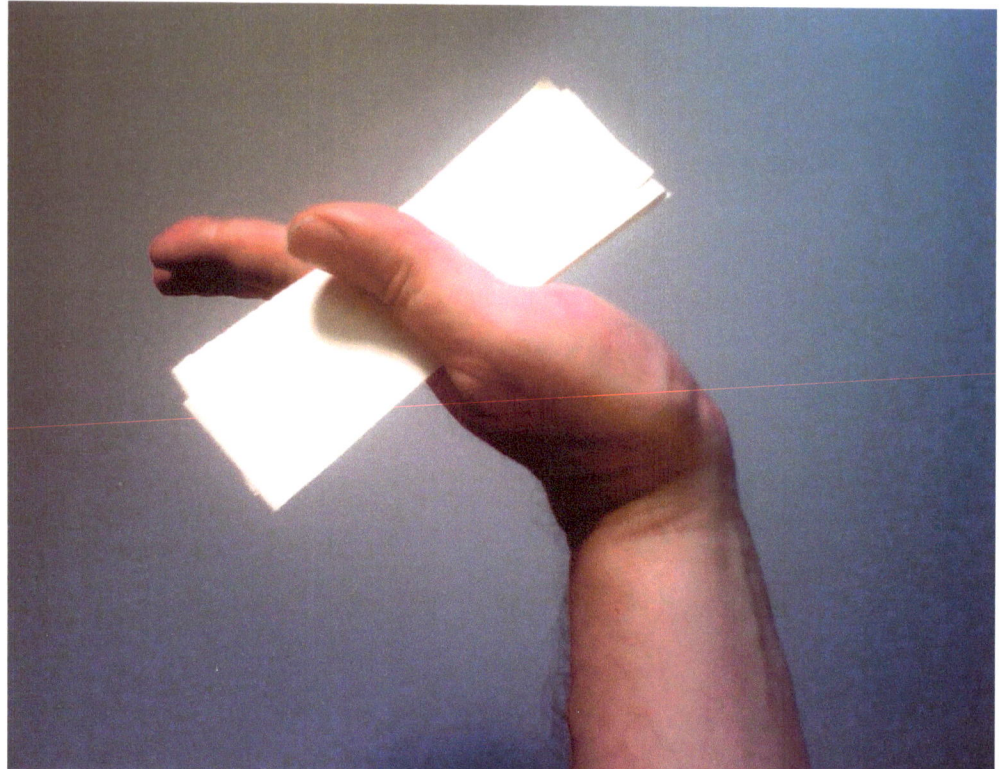

SIX- 19

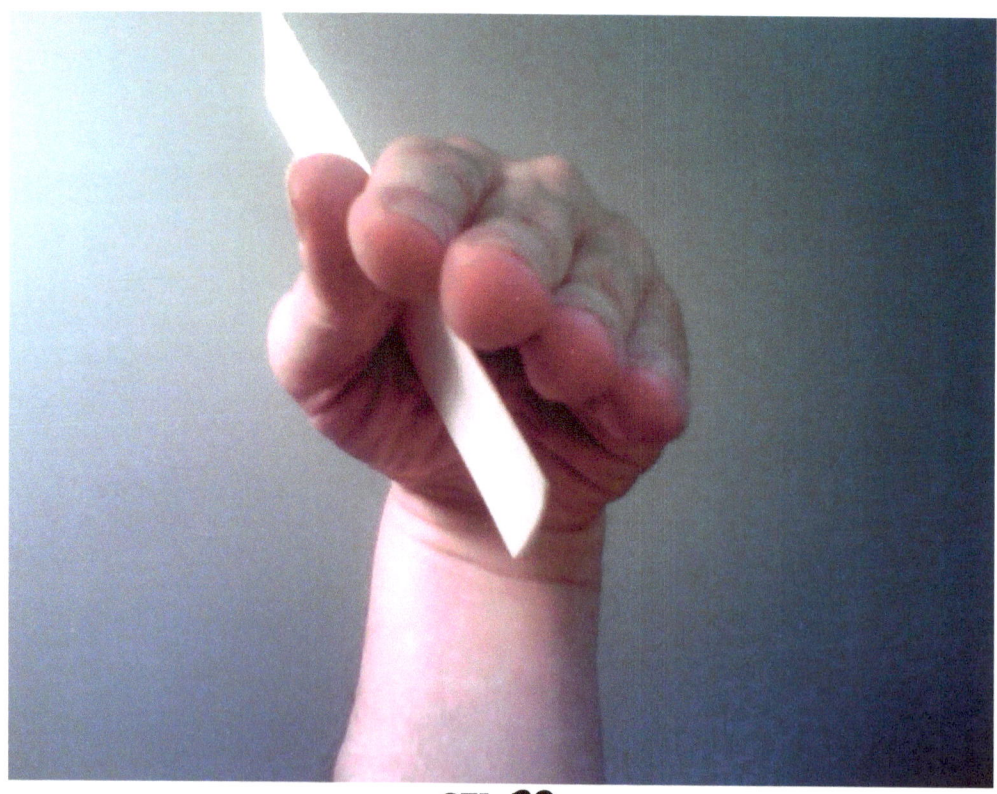

SIX - 20

"THE ORIGINAL" COWLING SYSTEM

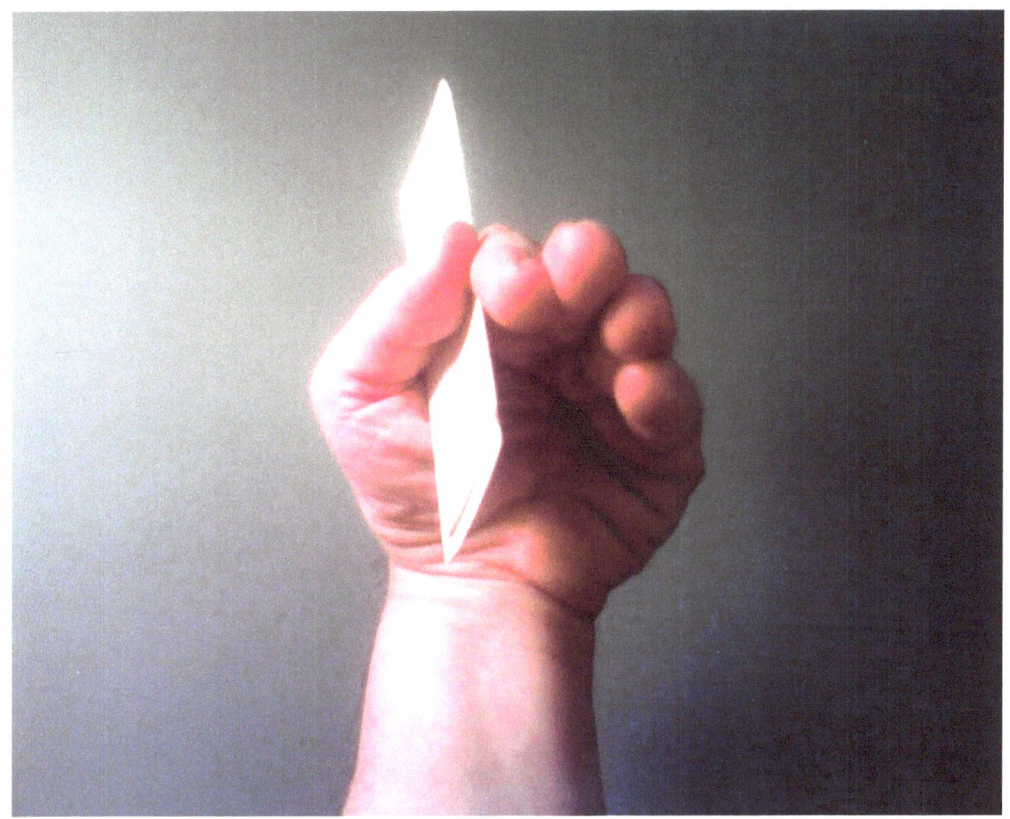

SIX - 21

LESSON SIX A

FOR DEVELOPING THE UPPER ARM, SHOULDER AND CHEST MUSCLES

The effect of this exercise is to expand the lungs, and to develop the biceps and triceps, and also the muscles of the chest and those between the shoulders. Incidentally it is a cure for 'round shoulders' because of the last-named effect.

The bedroom, with an open window and before dressing, gives the best conditions. If a cold bath is taken [and this is for the young and vigorous only, as a rule] the exercise should follow the bath as it will assist the reaction of the blood moving to the surface of the skin.

No apparatus is required, just some object by which to hold on: the rail of the bed is perhaps the best, but the back of a chair, the dressing table, or any substantial piece of furniture will suffice so long as it is about three to four feet from the floor and affords a stable grip for the hands.

Grasp the bed rail [or whatever you are using] with both hands about 2 feet apart, arms straight. Then bend the arms, moving forward with the body, elbows pointing outwards, until the chest almost touches the object you are gripping. Then in one continuous movement, straighten the arms, which will return your body to the almost-vertical position.

Inhale through the nose as you go forward, exhale strongly as you straighten up. Keep the feet firmly in place on the floor, making the ankles the hinge of the movement.

For the first three days, do this exercise three or four times in succession, gradually increasing to ten times towards the end of the week. The rate of movement should be about one forward movement per second, then one backward movement per second. Therefore, if you the whole cycle ten times, the entire exercise takes less than 1/2 a minute.

It is a good start for the day, especially on cold mornings, and is well worth doing **every** morning. **[editors note; This particular exercise does NOT have to be dropped after the end of the week, but may be continued indefinitely, along with the hand exercise[s] for each week.]**

"THE ORIGINAL" COWLING SYSTEM

LESSON SEVEN

EXERCISING THE FIRST JOINTS
[NO PHOTOGRAPHS]

So far we have considered developing the hand by movements from the second and third joints only. We must now consider the independent movement of the first phalange [the segment of the finger farthest from the wrist], and from now onwards the following exercise should be practiced for five minutes every day, immediately preceding one of the ten minute periods of practice of the progressive [main] lesson.

The intention will be better understood if we imagine a metal or wooden sheath which would completely encircle the finger between the "webbing" and the first joint, binding the finger tightly at the middle joints so as to prevent movement at this point but leaving the top portion - the first phalange - unbound and free to move.

Considering that you are working on the left hand, grasp the first finger with the thumb of the right hand in front of the finger, and the first and second fingers of the right hand behind it, so that the member being operated upon is restrained from bending at the second [or middle] joint.

The right hand thumbnail will be just below the line indicating the first joint, and the right hand first and second fingers will act as the restrainer at the back of the first finger. The best position is to hold the hand sideways, with the thumb pointing towards the face.

If may be necessary to read these preceding instructions more than once in order to understand what is intended. When all is quite clear the actual exercises should then be tried.

THE EXERCISE:

Slowly bend the first phalange and hold it in the bent position for five seconds, then straighten and relax for two seconds. Bend again and relax, and so on for five times. Then proceed in like manner with the second, third, and fourth fingers, and afterwards change over and do the exercise with the right hand fingers similarly.

Initially not much movement of this first phalange may be possible, but after a little practice, greater facility will be gained, until quite an appreciable portion of the arc of the circle is covered by the movement.

The effect of this exercise is to stretch the corresponding ligament, creating greater speed and responsiveness, adding to the "hammering power" of the fingers appreciably.

LESSON SEVEN - Cont'd

Another effect is to "slim" thick fingers, an effect which is particularly appreciated by pianists who have fleshy fingers and consequent difficulty in playing in-between the black keys.

Many students report that when doing the exercises of Lesson One, the first phalange automatically bends as the finger is being bent at the middle joint. A little practice of the above exercise will develop a certain amount of control over this first phalange. This has a special application for violinists, for very rapid passages are best produced by *flat* fingers, the first phalange not being bent.

Once again, the warning against being over-strenuous: The "golden rule" is to stop exercising immediately if the hand or fingers begin to feel tired. Be content with quite a small movement of the first phalange initially, and after doing the exercise with either hand, follow on with:

A FURTHER EXERCISE FOR DEVELOPING FINGER INDEPENDENCE

[ONE PHOTOGRAPH, #22, AND
PHOTOGRAPH #1, SENT WITH LESSON ONE, ALSO TO BE USED]

This may be considered as affording a complete relaxation from the one you have just done:

Hold the hand as in photo **#1**. Then, keeping the fingers quite flat, separate the 2nd and 3rd fingers as widely as possible without strain, as in photo **#22** and hold in this position until the fingers show a tendency to return to their normal position 'by themselves'

When this occurs, relax the entire hand for half a minute, and repeat as before, alternating with the right hand so as not to cause undue fatigue. The length of time which it takes before this tendency of the fingers to return to the normal position should be noted **[you can use the 60 BPM metronome click]** and an endeavor made to retain the position for 5 seconds longer the following day.

For example; if, on the first attempt it is possible to retain the position for 20 seconds, then the next day, try to retain the position for 25 seconds, the day after that, 30 seconds, etc., until the fingers can be kept apart for a full minute.

As before, concentrate fully and closely on what you are doing.

"THE ORIGINAL" COWLING SYSTEM 33

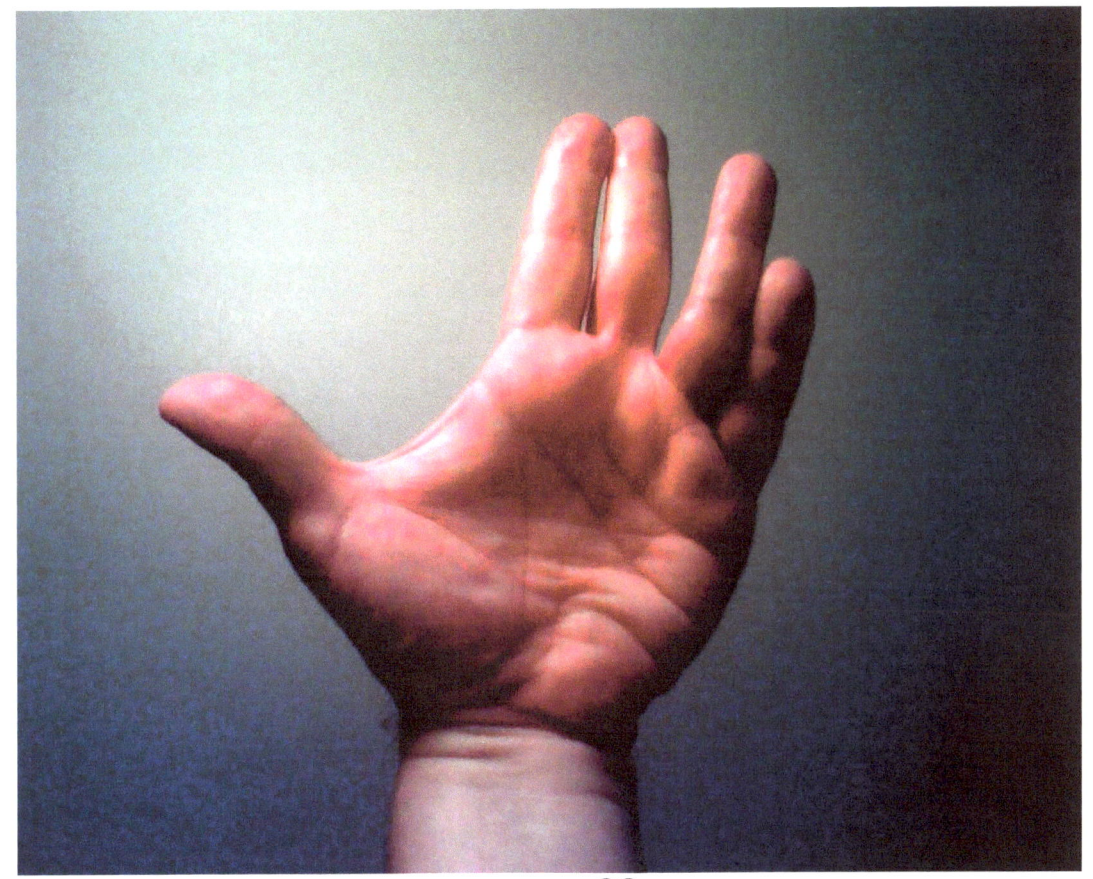

SEVEN - 22

LESSON EIGHT

TO DEVELOP INDEPENDENCE OF FINGERING

ONE NEW PHOTOGRAPH - #21A
PHOTOS #2 & #17 [ON PREVIOUS PAGES, TO BE USED ALSO]

The photographs show the left hand. Each hand is to be exercised separately, as per usual.

Hold the hand as in photo **#2**.

Extend the first finger as much as possible without strain, as in photo **#17**, retaining the position for 10 seconds.

Bend the first finger from the middle joint only, the other three fingers being kept perfectly straight, and endeavor to keep it well separated from the other fingers as in photo **#21a**, retain this position for 10 seconds.

Resume the position as in photo **#2**.

Extend the fourth finger in a similar way to the first finger in photo **#21b** and retain it in this position for 10 seconds.

Now bend the fourth finger from the middle joint as in photo **#21c**, keeping it well separated from the other fingers and retaining it in this position for 10 seconds.

[ed. note:"Resume the position as in photo #2." is not present in the original instructions at this step, but it is assumed to be the final position in the cycle]

Practice six of seven times with the left hand, then with the right, and continue in this fashion for ten minutes. Repeat this entire exercise only after a minimum interval of two hours, for another ten minutes.

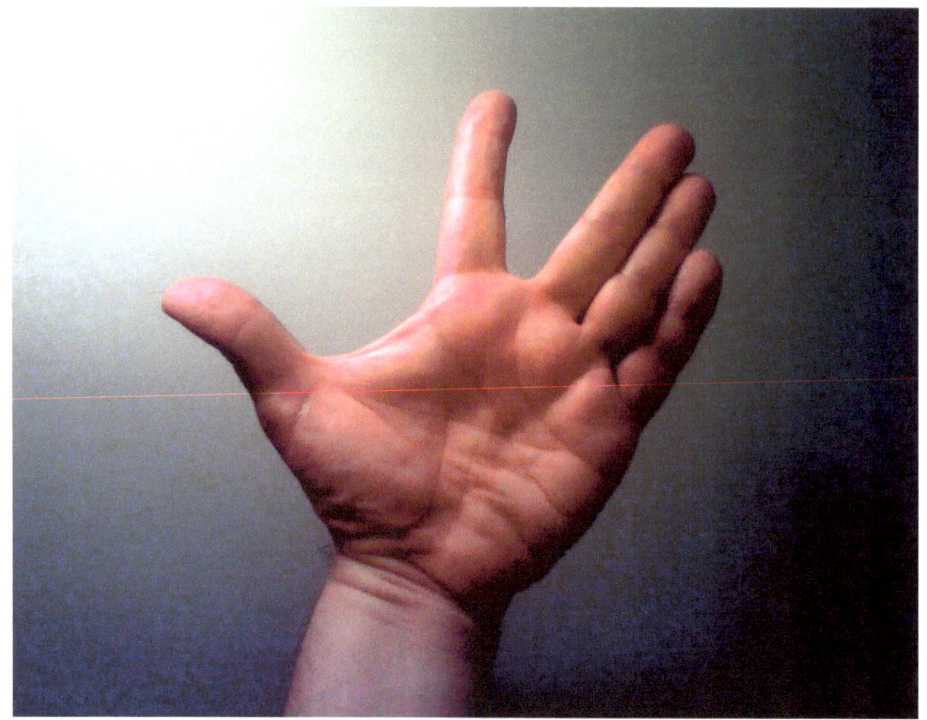
EIGHT — 17 [SAME POSITION AS IN LESSON FIVE]

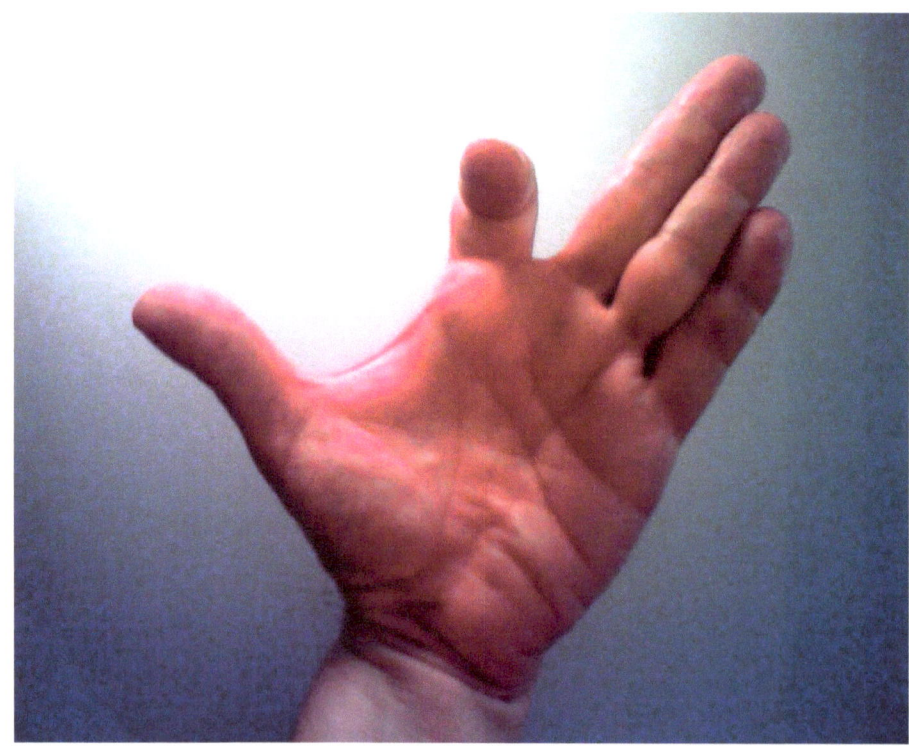
EIGHT - 21A

"THE ORIGINAL" COWLING SYSTEM 37

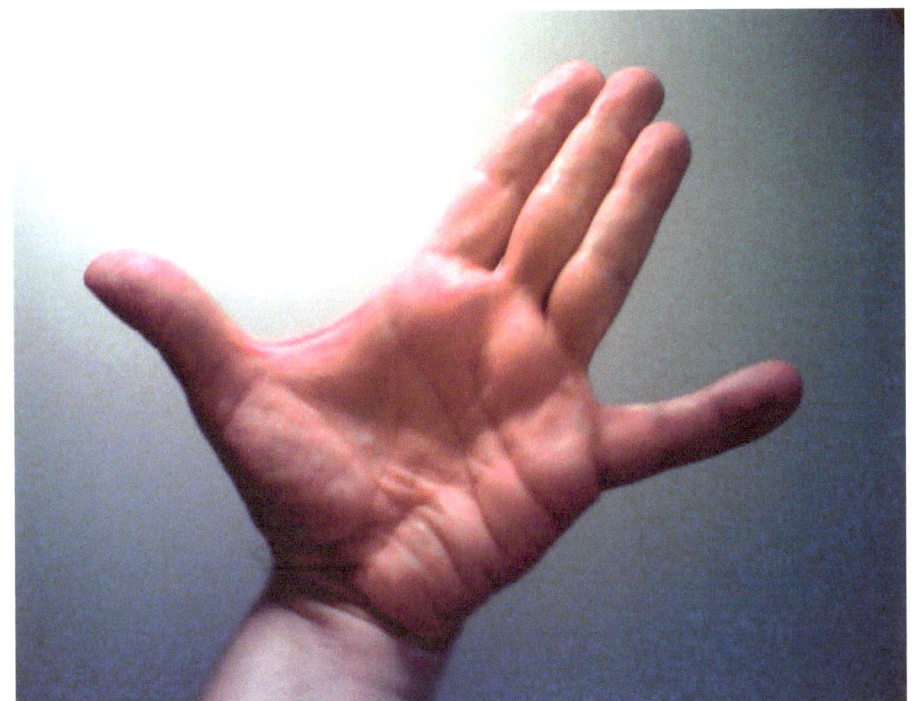

EIGHT 21 B

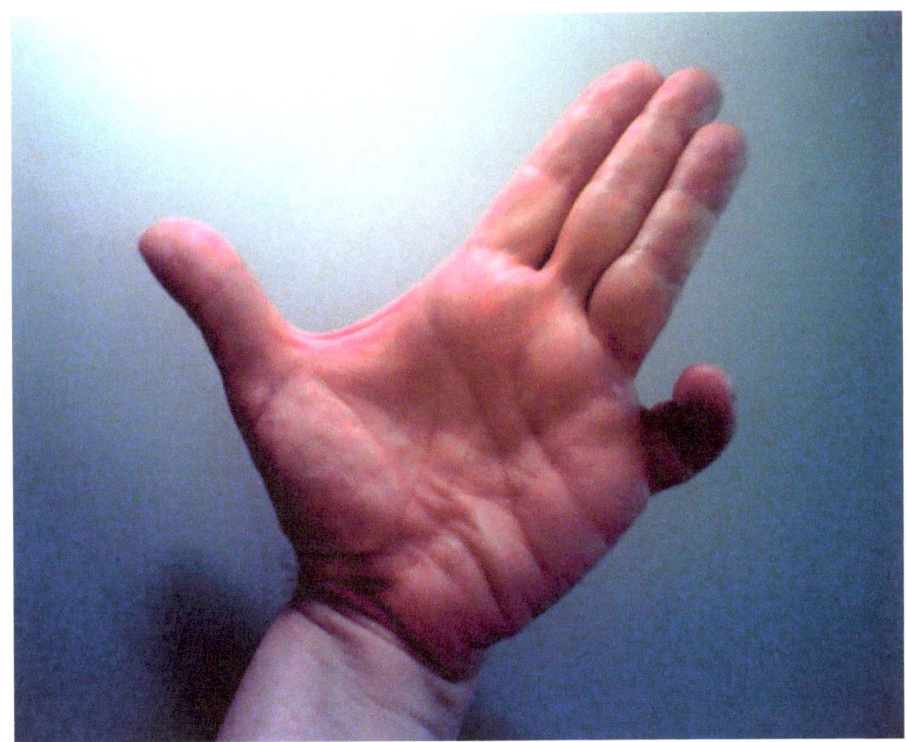

EIGHT - 21 C

"THE ORIGINAL" COWLING SYSTEM 39

LESSON NINE

COMBINED EXERCISE FOR THIRD JOINTS AND WRISTS

[Four photos, #'s 30, 31, 32, 33]

The photographs show the left hand. As in previous lessons, the exercise is to be practiced with the right also.

By this time you should have developed a fair amount of strength in all the finger joints and the wrists, and should be ready for this somewhat strenuous exercise.

Carefully note the effects, which will be felt in the wrist and forearm, and *if the sensation of fatigue is at all excessive, change the exercise from one hand to the other on the completion of every third movement, and retain the hand in the various positions for 5 seconds only, instead of ten, and without clenching the hand tightly.* Do this for the first three days, after which the exercise may be followed according the instructions below:

FIRST POSITION: Elbow close to the side, the hand about a foot from the shoulder and a little below the level of the shoulder, clench the hand, but not too tightly, and hold in position as in photo **#30** for a count of 10 seconds.

SECOND POSITION: Raise the knuckles from the third joint only, until the middle joints, third joints and back of the hand are quite in line and perfectly flat, as in photo **#31**, and retain this position for 10 seconds.

THIRD POSITION: Turn the hand smartly towards you at the same time clenching the hand as in photo **#32**, not too tensely, and retain for 10 seconds.

FOURTH POSITION: Raise the knuckles from the third joint, as in photo **#33**, and hold the position for 10 seconds. In this position the fingers are spaced such as to allow a pencil to fit between the tips of the fingers and the palm of the hand.

Retain each position for ten seconds before proceeding to the next; repeat the entire sequence 6 times, then change to the right hand. Practice for 10 minutes twice daily, with the usual minimum wait of two hours between exercising.

Particular care must be taken not to overstrain, and the warnings regarding concentration of the attention, as given in previous lessons, must be strictly observed.

The previous lesson should now be discontinued.

40 "THE ORIGINAL" COWLING SYSTEM

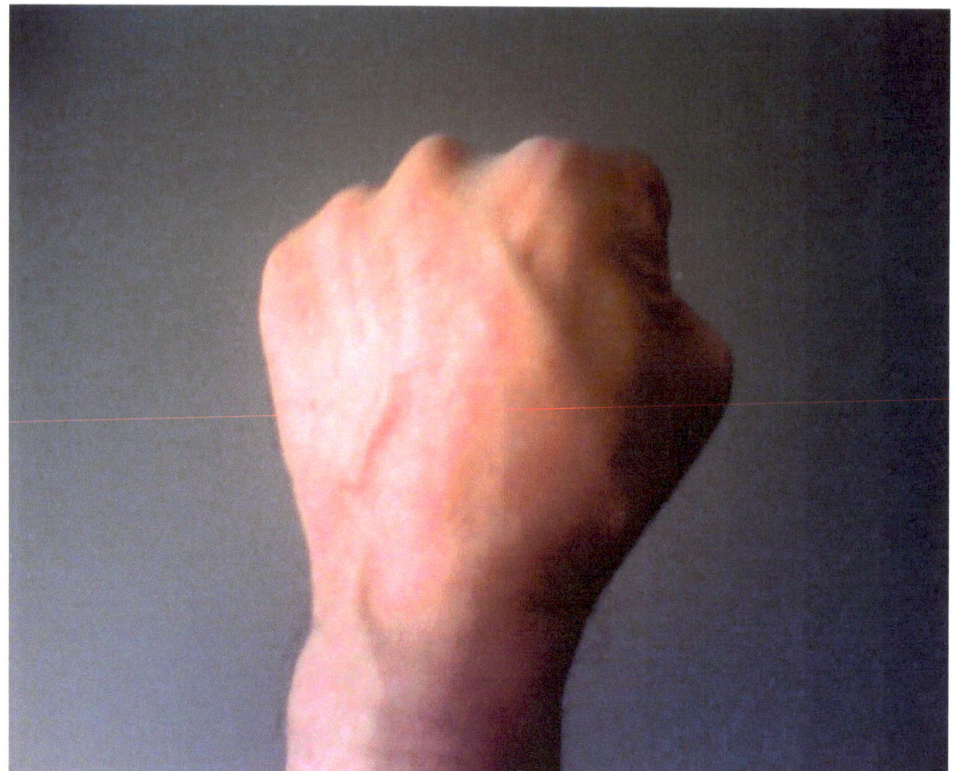

NINE - 30

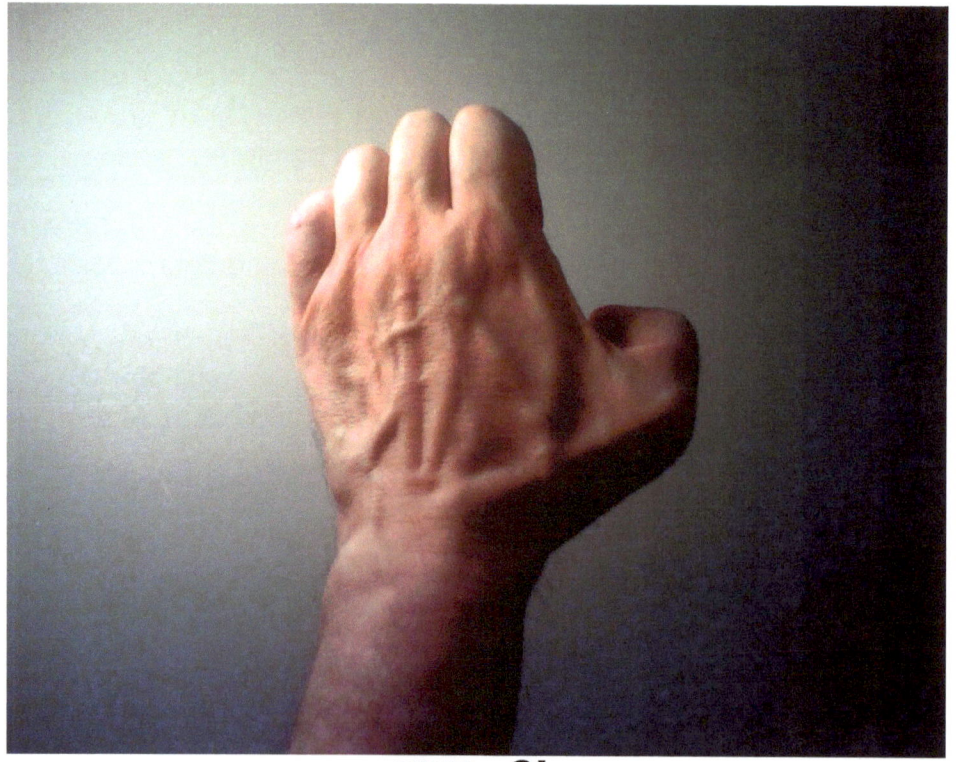

NINE — 31

"THE ORIGINAL" COWLING SYSTEM 41

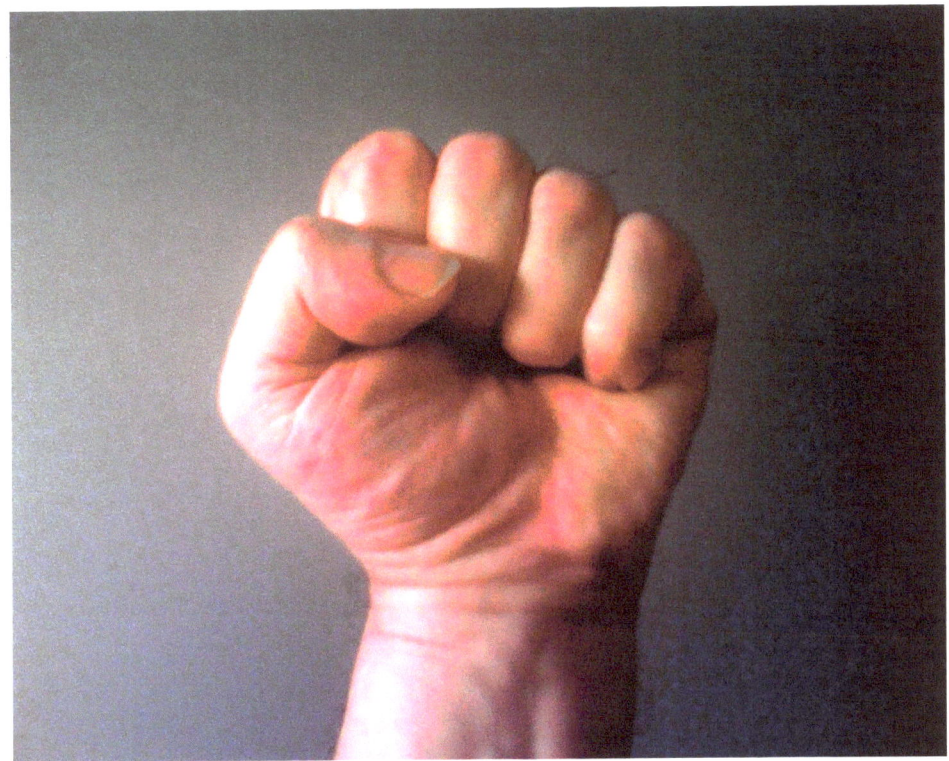

NINE — 32

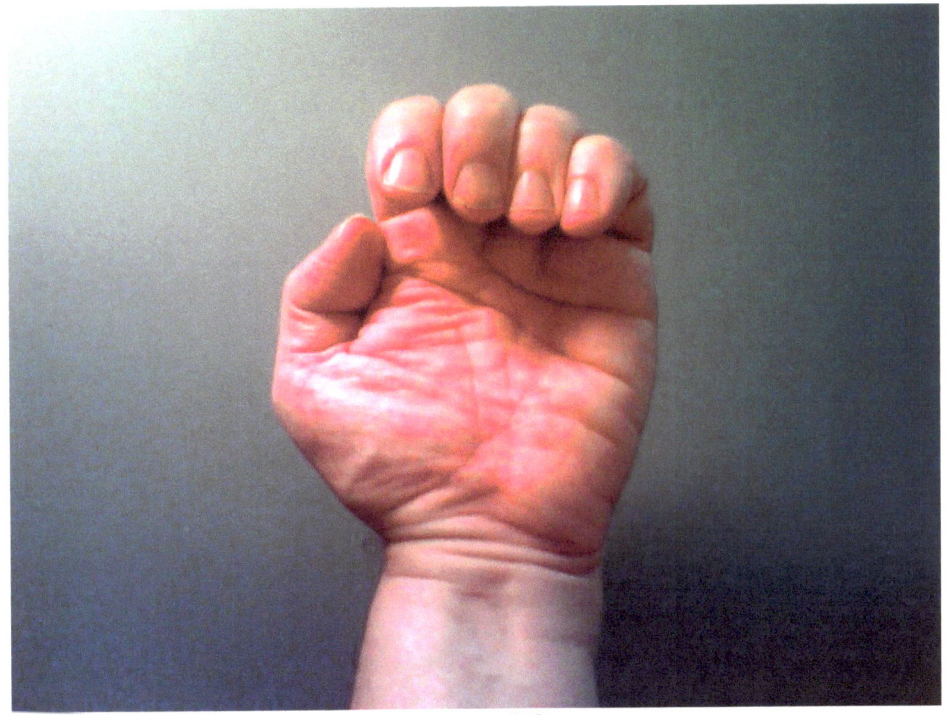

NINE - 33

THE OCTAVE PLAYING EXERCISE

The difficulty in playing octaves on the piano is invariably due to weakness of the wrist, and as a result, the hand and arm become tired very quickly. In accordance with the principles of the Cowling System, therefore, the remedy is to develop and strengthen the muscles and 'supple' the ligaments which surround the small bones of the wrist by the movements shown in the accompanying photographs - until the action which takes place when playing octaves on the piano cam be maintained for five or ten minutes continuously without any fatigue.

EXPLANATION of the accompanying photographs: Take a piece of wood and cut it down until it is exactly 5 3/4" in length [which is slightly under the width of an octave on the piano]. The diameter of the stick is not important - an unsharpened lead pencil of this length would serve.

Bridge the span between the thumb and little finger with this stick [see diagram **'OCTAVE EXERCISE I'** - a front view of the hand indicating the correct position] and hold with sufficient pressure to keep it in position.

Lay the right arm on the table with the whole hand projecting over the edge [see photographs], then grasp the right wrist firmly with the left hand to from a support, the thumb of the latter being uppermost. The grasp of the left hand round the wrist must not be too tight, as this would interfere with the circulation, or too near the wrist joints, as this would prevent free movement.

FIRST MOVEMENT: Raise hand to the limit of movement allowed by wrist, but without any strain, as shown in diagram **'OCTAVE EXERCISE II'**, and retain this position for five seconds.

SECOND MOVEMENT: Change to the position shown in diagram **'OCTAVE EXERCISE III'**. Hold this position for five seconds, then return to the position in diagram **'OCTAVE EXERCISE II'**, and repeat.

After six up-and-down movements with the right hand, change the stick to the left hand and repeat the movements similarly. The change from position II to position III is not done quickly, but should take about one second.

Remember that the essence of this, as it is with all the Cowling exercises, is the concentration of the mind upon the operation. *The exercise should be discontinued immediately if the hand begins to feel tired,* for it is somewhat strenuous; but in any case the exercise should <u>not</u> be continued for longer than **ten minutes, total.**

Before practicing this exercise, do the following self-test: Play octaves on the piano until the hand begins to feel tired and note how soon this occurs. [Use the metronome, etc.. – ed.] Then, after you have practiced the above exercises with the stick for a week do the self-test again. You should find that you can continue playing octaves on the piano for at least twice as long as you could seven days previously!

Editors note: The above exercise was additionally enclosed in the Lesson Nine envelope. You will note that the customary instructions to discontinue an exercise after one week aren't stated here. We assume therefore that one may now do this exercize with the others.

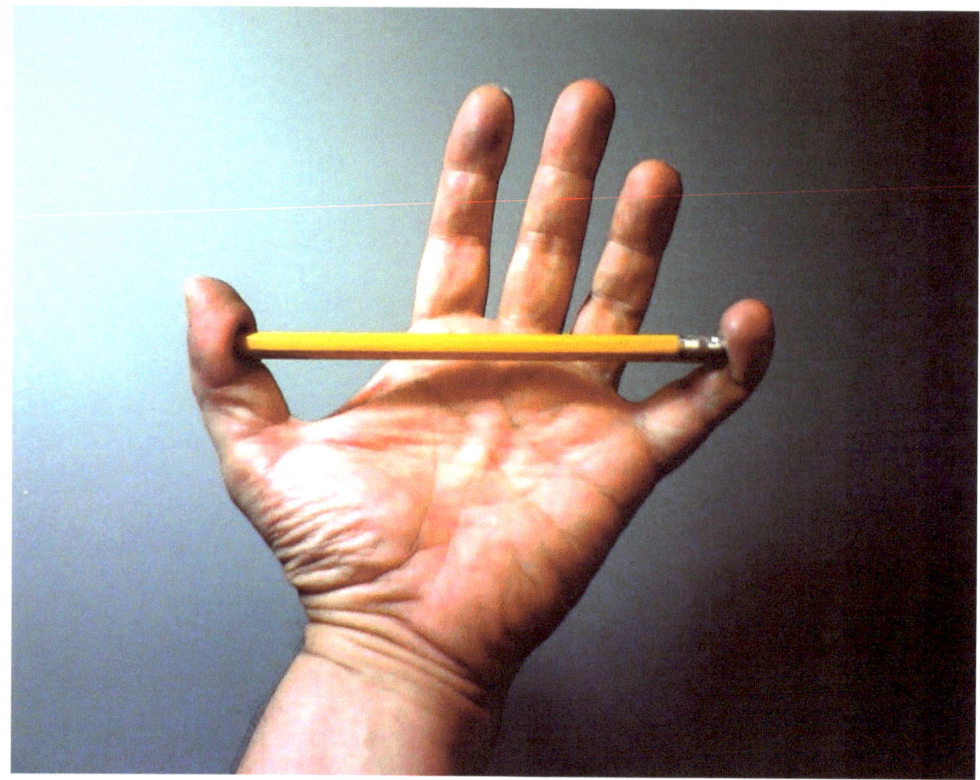

OCTAVE EXERCISE I

"THE ORIGINAL" COWLING SYSTEM 45

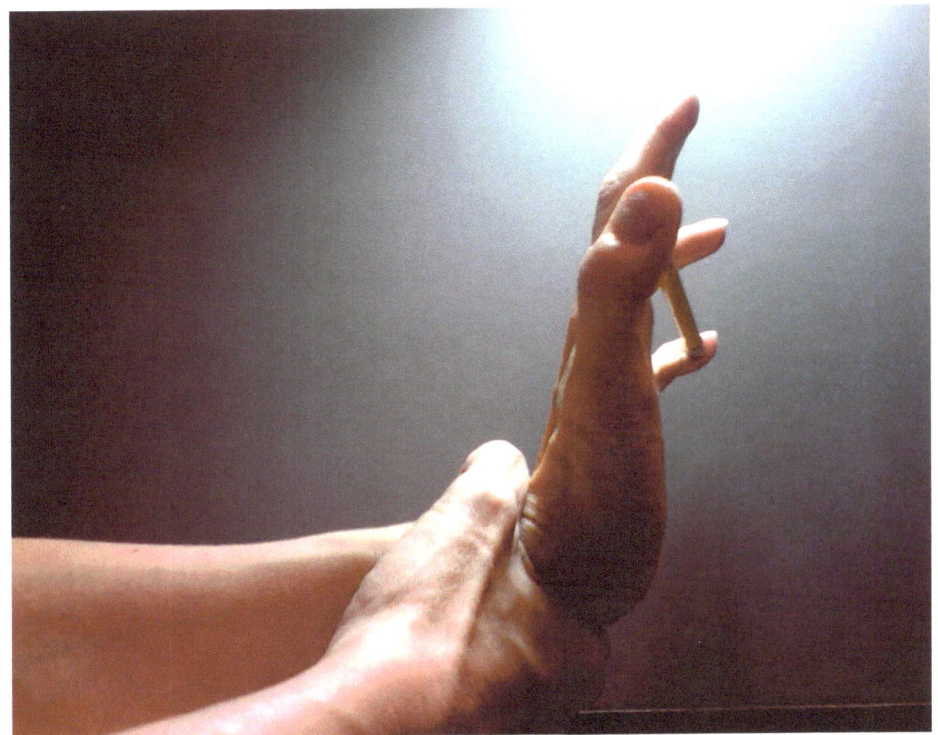

OCTAVE EXERCISE II

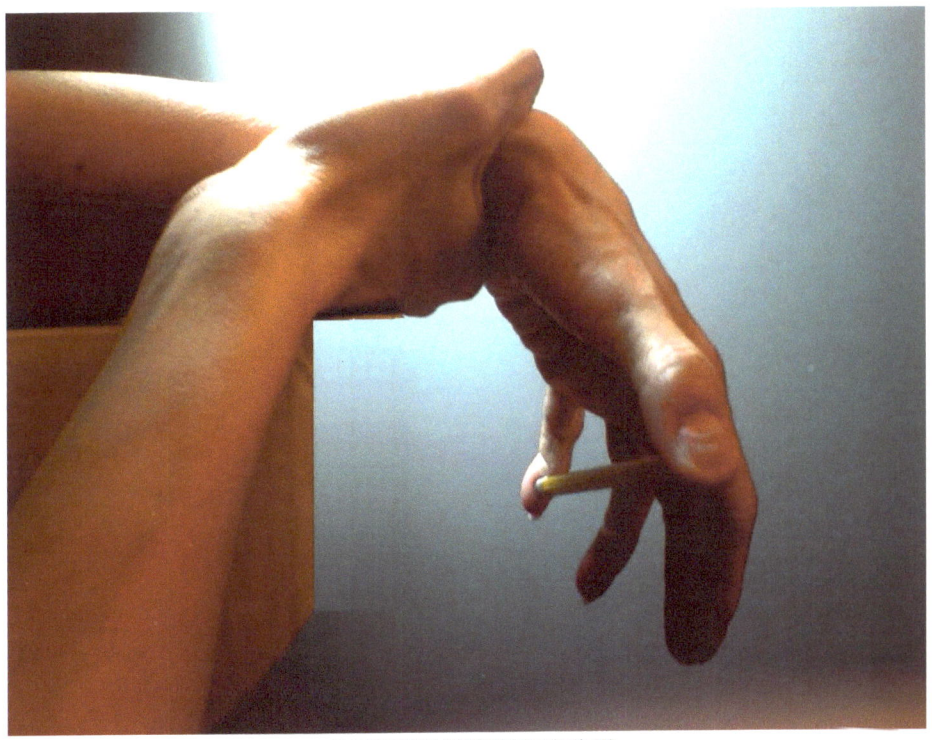

OCTAVE EXERCISE III

"THE ORIGINAL" COWLING SYSTEM

LESSON 10

POWER IN THE FOURTH FINGER!

FOR TRILLS, TURNS, SHAKES, AND EXTENDED MOVEMENTS FOR OCTAVE PLAYING

[TWO PHOTOGRAPHS ENCLOSED: #34 & #35,
ALSO PHOTOGRAPH #1 IS REFERRED TO]

The photographs show the left hand, but the exercise is to be practiced first with the left hand, then with the right - one hand at a time, never both together.

The effects of this exercise are often most marked, the fourth finger becoming perceptibly stronger every day, and in the opinion of many instrumentalists, this is one of the most valuable exercises in the series. Some care will be required to attain the correct positions and initially it may not be possible to get the fourth finger as far over as is shown in photo **#35**.

Note that the fourth finger is not touching the ball of the thumb, although it may appear so from the photograph because of the line of sight - the finger should be kept almost straight.

As an exception, The student may continue this exercise for five minutes every day while occupied with next week's lesson, 11. To be able to extend the fourth finger to the position shown in photo **#35** is a great advantage when playing trills, turns, shakes and octaves.

The effect of this exercise is to stretch the ligament which connects the fourth finger to a point near the elbow. If done too strenuously, a slight ache may be experienced between these two points, therefore a certain amount of caution and restraint is called for during the first few periods of practice.

FIRST POSITION: as in photo **#1** "**First Position**", hold for ten seconds.

SECOND POSITION: as in photo **#34**, the fingers bent in a natural attitude, without any effort to "place" them. Hold for ten seconds.

THIRD POSITION: as in photo **#35**, the fourth finger being stretched as far as possible over the ball of the thumb, the thumb itself being bent at the first joint, and the wrist being turned to the left as far as possible without strain.

LESSON TEN, CONT'D

It will be understood that the latter note applies when the left hand is being exercised - the wrist is turned to the right when the right hand is being exercised. In this photo, #35, the thumb and finger are not touching each other but are as far apart as possible. This position should be retained for ten seconds, the hand relaxed for the same period, then the exercise is done "mirror-image wise", with the right hand, as per usual. It is advised to alternate between left and left hands after each movement as this exercise is somewhat tiring.

On no account should the hand be held or turned with the other hand.

Practice for ten minutes morning and night, and continue to follow the principle of concentration, which is essential to the best result. The previous exercise may now be discontinued.

"THE ORIGINAL" COWLING SYSTEM 49

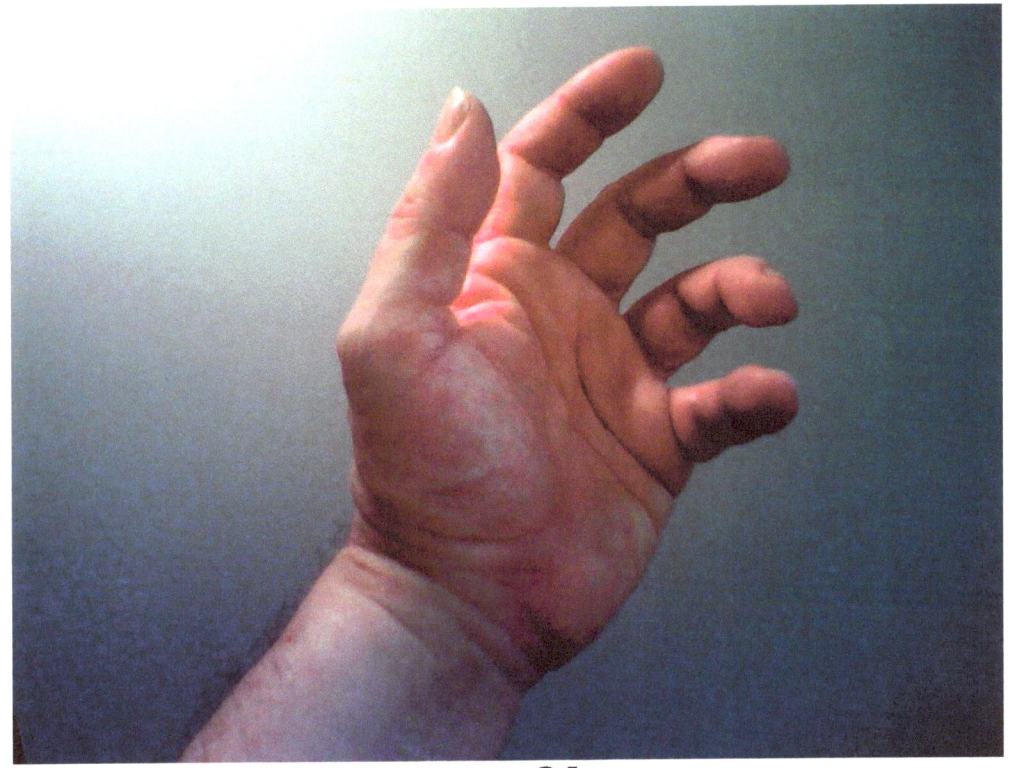

TEN - 34

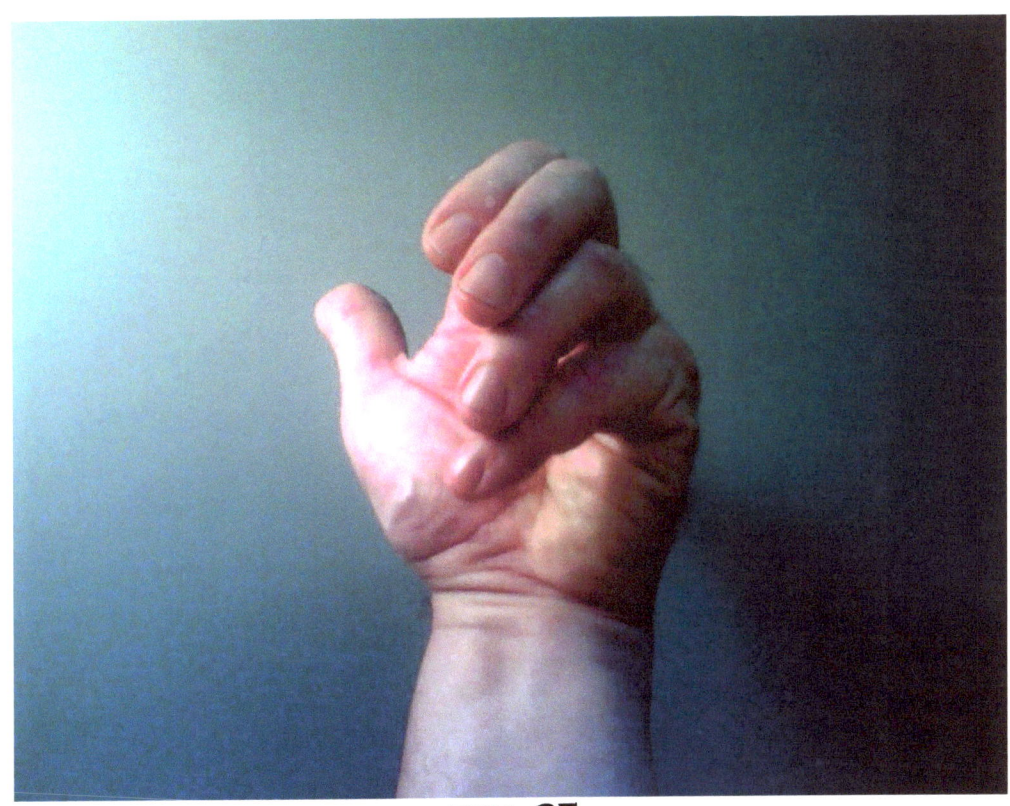

TEN - 35

"THE ORIGINAL" COWLING SYSTEM   51

LESSON ELEVEN

THUMB-UNDER EXCERCISE

[Photos #36, 37, 38]

The photographs show the left hand - as in all previous exercises however, the exercise must be practiced only with one hand at a time.

FIRST POSITION: Hold the hand as in photo **#36**, bent a little backward from the wrist.

SECOND POSITION: As in photo **#37**, the thumb, and also the fingers, being kept quite straight, and the fingers extended as shown. Retain in this position for **TWELVE** seconds [*not ten* as with the previous exercises].

THIRD POSITION: Keeping the other two fingers well back, bend the **first and third** finger as in photo **#38**, and hold for **TWELVE** seconds.

FOURTH POSITION: [no photograph] Bend the **second** and **fourth** fingers, straightening the first and third, and keep in this position for **TWELVE** seconds.

During these movements, the thumb must not be allowed to bend, but must be kept perfectly straight along both joints. The movements copy those which take place when playing the piano, violin, cello [and guitar and bass], but with this difference: that the mind is occupied only with the hand itself, instead of the hands, the music, the audience, etc. and the retention of the various positions for twelve seconds at a time ensures the thorough exercise of the muscles involved.

Practice for ten minutes, once in the AM and once in the PM.

52   "THE ORIGINAL" COWLING SYSTEM

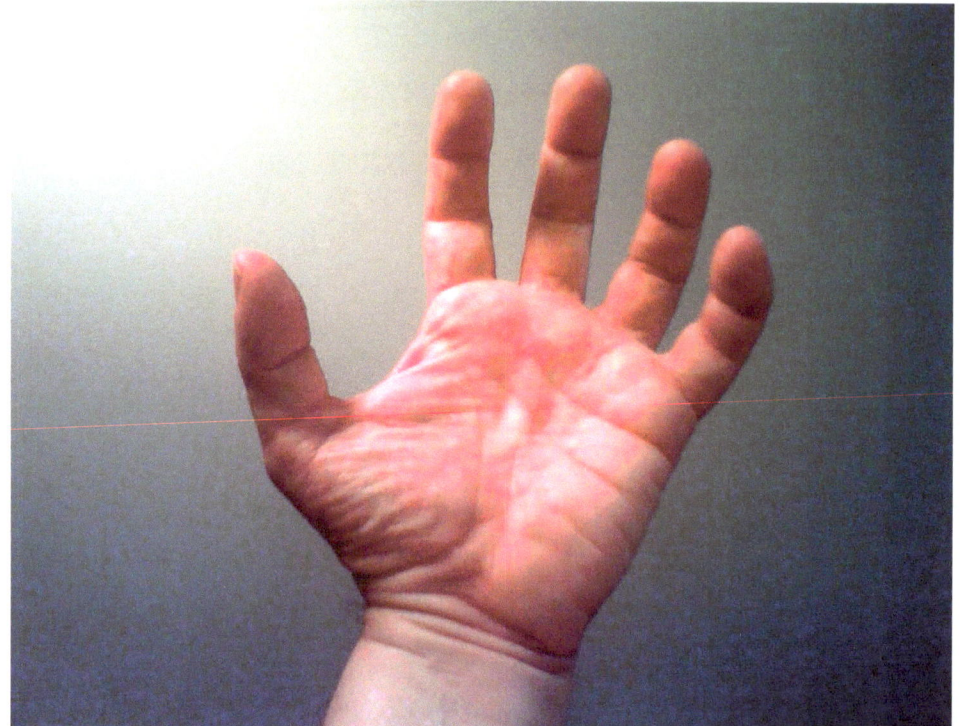

ELEVEN - 36

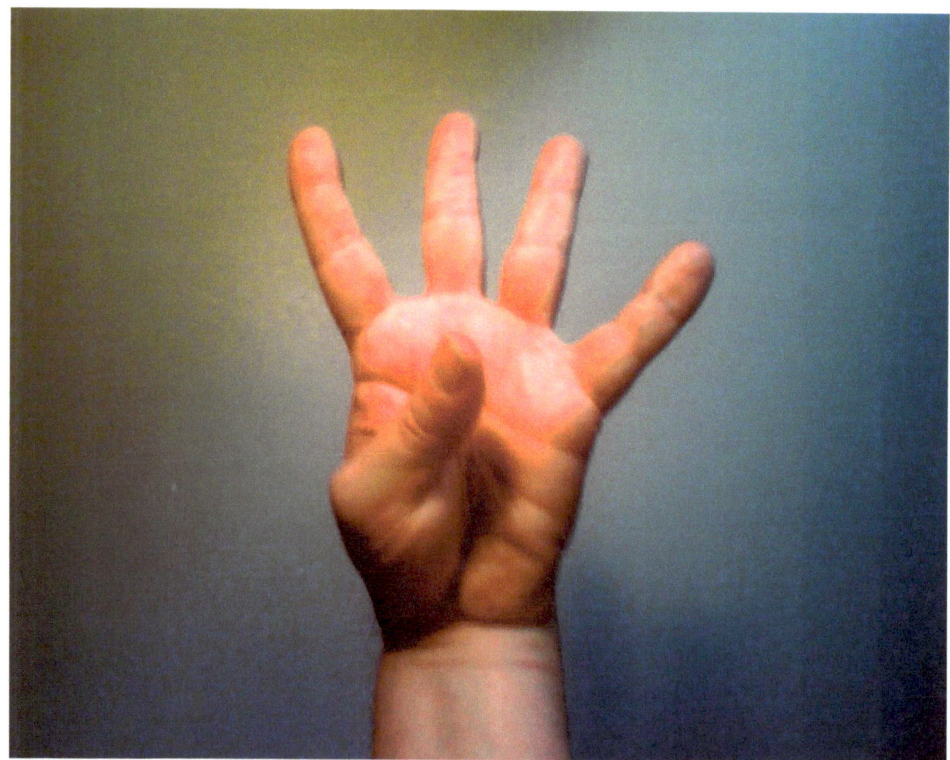

ELEVEN - 37

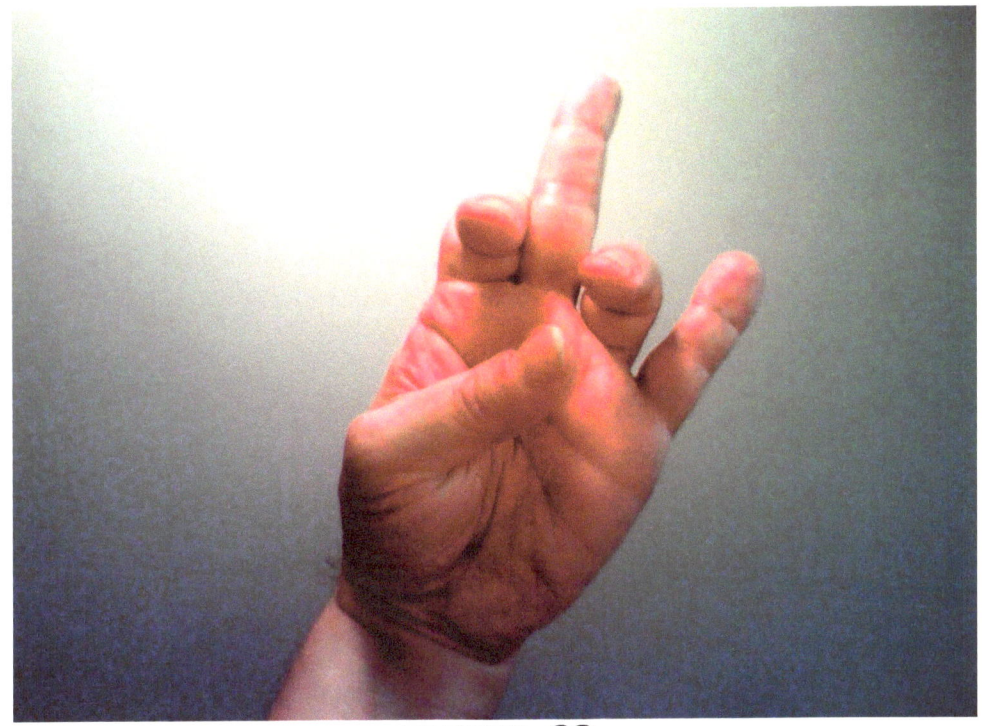

ELEVEN - 38

CONGRATULATIONS!

YOU HAVE COMPLETED THE FULL BATTERY OF COWLING SYSTEM EXERCISES!

IT IS NOW SUGGESTED THAT YOU START AT THE <u>FIRST</u> LESSON AND GO THROUGH THEM ALL AGAIN IN ORDER. YOU MAY [AND SHOULD] <u>PERSIST</u> IN PRACTICING THE COWLING EXERCISES TO YOUR CONTINUED BENEFIT.

ALSO:

IF YOU HAVE EXPERIENCED AN INCREASE OF SPEED, STRENGTH AND DEXTERITY AND WISH TO SHARE YOUR SUCCESSES USING THE COWLING SYSTEM, PLEASE FEEL FREE TO CONTACT US, AT

http://www.facebook.com/pages/The-Original-Cowling-System/147646368595612?v=wall

OR:

http://www.make-music-better.com/contact-us.html

THANK YOU VERY MUCH FOR YOUR PARTICIPATION!

RAVE REVIEWS FOR "THE ORIGINAL" COWLING SYSTEM©

"**Many** thanks for the lessons I have received. I must say that I am highly delighted with the way my fingering has improved since I commenced your hand exercises. Recently I became very despondent about my violin playing and almost inclined to give it up, but now I feel it a pleasure, thanks to the *Cowling System*." ~ "The Violinist" Magazine: December, 1924

"**I am** a guitarist, I have played guitar since 1964. Self taught, I reached an "A" level in music in 1989. I was introduced to the *Cowling System* by a violinist in his seventies, who had amazing dexterity on his instrument for his age. (He had sent away for the course in the 1930's.) I would, and have, recommended this system to *anyone* wanting to improve their dexterity on *any* instrument. I have been using the exercises since the 1980's and believe me ***they work***." ~ Don Wills

"**I find** it remarkable that such a system that made a world of difference in my piano playing as a teenager had disappeared. In 1976, my teacher gave me his copy of all the exercises, whereupon I made xeroxed pages to put in a binder. *My teacher was amazed at my progress that in a year I could play, for example, the prelude #17 of Chopin!* ~ "rpn58" [from a pianists' discussion board]

YOUR SEARCH FOR A TECHNIQUE BREAKTHROUGH STOPS HERE!

THESE ARE THE HAND STRENGTHENING EXERCISES FOR MUSICIANS, WHICH REALLY DO WORK.
TRY "THE ORIGINAL" COWLING SYSTEM© AND SEE.

Artistic Production Services
New York City, NY - Visit us at:

http://www.make-music-better.com/contact-us.html

ISBN 978-0-615-17050-3

www.ingramcontent.com/pod-product-compliance
Lightning Source LLC
Chambersburg PA
CBHW041702160426
43191CB00003B/54